# Date Due

# FORMS OF LYRIC

# Forms of Lyric

SELECTED PAPERS FROM THE
ENGLISH INSTITUTE

EDITED WITH A FOREWORD
BY REUBEN A. BROWER

COLUMBIA UNIVERSITY PRESS · NEW YORK AND LONDON

*1970*

PR
509
.L8
B8

82[.09
E58

COPYRIGHT © 1970 COLUMBIA UNIVERSITY PRESS
ISBN: 0-231-03413-X
LIBRARY OF CONGRESS CATALOG CARD NUMBER: 78-121567
PRINTED IN THE UNITED STATES OF AMERICA

ACKNOWLEDGMENTS

Acknowledgment is gratefully made to the following for permission to quote from copyrighted material: Faber and Faber, for permission to quote extracts from Theodore Roethke's "Meditation at Oyster River" and "The Far Field," from *The Far Field*. Doubleday & Company, for permission to quote extracts from Theodore Roethke's "Meditation at Oyster River" (copyright © 1960 by Beatrice Roethke, Administratrix of the Estate of Theodore Roethke) and an extract from Theodore Roethke's "The Far Field" (copyright © 1962 by Beatrice Roethke, Administratrix of the Estate of Theodore Roethke, both from *The Collected Poems of Theodore Roethke;* reprinted by permission of Doubleday & Company, Inc. Charles Tomlinson, Oxford University Press, and Ivan Obolensky, Inc., for permission to quote Mr. Tomlinson's "The Atlantic," from *Seeing Is Believing*. The Johns Hopkins Press, for permission to reprint the article "The Inevitable Ear: Freedom and Necessity in Lyric Form, Wordsworth and After," by Donald Wesling, which originally appeared in *ELH*, Vol. XXXVI, No. 3 (1969), pp. 544–61 (© The Johns Hopkins Press). Charles Scribner's Sons, for permission to quote Howard Moss's "The Pruned Tree" (copyright © 1963 Howard Moss), which first appeared in *The New Yorker* and is reprinted with permission of Charles Scribner's Sons from *Finding Them Lost*, by Howard Moss. Wesleyan University Press, for permission to quote extracts from James Wright's "A Blessing" (copyright © 1961 by James Wright), from *The Branch Will Not Break*, by James Wright

(Wesleyan University Press, Middletown, Conn., 1963). Holt, Rinehart and Winston, for permission to quote Robert Frost's "Never Again Would Birds' Song Be the Same," "The Lost Follower," and an extract from "I Could Give All to Time," from *The Poetry of Robert Frost*, edited by Edward Connery Lathem; copyright 1942 by Robert Frost; copyright © 1970 by Lesley Frost Ballantine; reprinted by permission of Holt, Rinehart and Winston, Inc. Eyre & Spottiswoode, Ltd., for permission to quote an extract from Randall Jarrell's "Next Day." The Macmillan Company, for permission to quote an extract from Randall Jarrell's "Next Day," published in *The Lost World*; reprinted with permission of The Macmillan Company; copyright © by Randall Jarrell, 1963; this poem originally appeared in *The New Yorker*. Atheneum Publishers, Inc., for permission to quote Randall Jarrell's "Aging," from *Woman at the Washington Zoo*, by Randall Jarrell; copyright 1954 © 1960 by Randall Jarrell; reprinted by permission of Atheneum Publishers; this poem originally appeared in *Poetry*. City Lights Books, for permission to quote an extract from Allen Ginsberg's "Poem Rocket," from *Kaddish and Other Poems*, copyright © 1961 by Allen Ginsberg; reprinted by permission of City Lights Books. Harper & Row, Publishers, Inc., for permission to quote an extract from Robert Bly's "Sleet Storm on the Merritt Parkway," from *The Light Around the Body*, by Robert Bly; copyright © 1962 by Robert Bly; by permission of Harper & Row, Publishers, Inc. Farrar, Straus & Giroux, Inc., for permission to quote Robert Lowell's "Skunk Hour," reprinted with the permission of Farrar, Straus & Giroux, Inc., from *Life Studies* by Robert Lowell, copyright © 1958 by Robert Lowell.

The essays that follow were presented (with one exception) at two conferences of the English Institute: the first, in 1968, on "Freedom and Necessity in the Lyric Form," directed by Professor Robert Langbaum; the second, in 1969, on "Forms of the Lyric," directed by the editor. It may be noted that in the transition from conference to publication, the article has disappeared from the title chosen for this volume, the loss reflecting an uneasiness shared by the editor and his colleagues. If "forms" comes trailing clouds of Platonism, "the" Lyric seems to suggest a Form indeed. Even in the plural, form is a troublesome term for a generation of critics who have rejected the traditional dichotomy of "form and content." But though most of us can get along quite happily without the second of the two terms, we can hardly talk for long about a poem and not use the first or one of its current equivalents—structure, pattern, design, order. While some of these more fashionable terms have the advantage of not being associated with "content," they are subject to the same abuses as other critical terms. We may not murder to dissect, but if we carry on any discourse about works of literature, we must direct attention to certain items abstracted from the whole. Whatever word we use to indicate that we are attending to "this in relation to this" and not "that in relation to that," there is always the possibility that we may freeze the life of the poem into lifeless formula.

The authors of these studies, it will be readily seen, have not succumbed to this temptation, while exercising complete freedom in their choice of terminology and method. Various as the essays are in subject and in emphasis, they are all characterized by flexibility in approach and by immediacy of response to the poems under consideration. Readers with a penchant for definition may amuse themselves with discovering the implied definitions of "form" or "lyric," or with challenging the more explicit ones. Two assumptions may be pointed out as common to most, if not all, of the contributors: the view of structure as event, as observed order in the experience of reading a poem, and the view of poetic composition as a "form of proceeding" —to use the Coleridgean expression adopted in one of the essays. In another, we read of "the sense of order in the poem"; in a third, of the poet's "way of conducting a poem" and of his "re-invention as he goes along"; in a fourth, of "the figure a poem makes." Coleridge, it appears, is still the presiding genius of twentieth-century criticism of poetry.

The essays are arranged in chronological order, and they have been selected to show how poets of different periods have "found their form," have struck out their individual way between imitation and freedom of "conducting a poem." The collection as a whole, though hardly constituting a history of poetry, illustrates some of the ways in which the history of poetry is in the process of being rewritten. Again it should be emphasized that freedom is the keynote: the writers make it abundantly clear that changing forms of lyric demand changing forms of criticism of lyric.

REUBEN A. BROWER

*Harvard University*
*January, 1970*

# CONTENTS

# FORMS OF LYRIC

G. K. HUNTER

# Drab and Golden Lyrics

# of the Renaissance

TO begin to write about "the lyrics of the English Renaissance" is, I have discovered, to imply so many presuppositions that all the following pages might be spent in taking the title to pieces. I should like to avoid such a self-defeating exercise. But I must comment on at least one assumption—that the lyrics of the period can be usefully subsumed under a single descriptive heading. It might well be alleged that the only legitimate distinction is between good lyrics and bad lyrics, and that good lyrics are not members of a class but individual poems whose goodness is their only common feature. I have much sympathy with this point of view. But I remember that critics exist to make good art more available to the public, and that the relation of good poems of a period to one another is an effective way of making such poems more available. So I should like to be able to begin by writing about the Renaissance lyric in England as if such a thing existed.

Some ways of relating poems are, however, difficult to apply in this period. Modern poems are usually assumed to cluster in a convenient way around the minds of their authors. This elementary critical convenience will work for some writers of the time—Sidney, Wyatt, Ralegh, for example—but a great mass of its lyrics are anonymous. Even when we have an author's name we do not necessarily have the coherence of a personality to contain or relate the divergencies of individual poems. What critical handle to appreciation is given by the information that Henry Chettle wrote "Diaphenia like the daffadowndilly"? How far is our response to "His golden locks time hath to silver turned" affected by the supposition that Sir Henry Lee rather than George Peele wrote the poem?

Adventitious critical interest may sometimes be attached to individual poems by biographical speculation. We may (if we wish) assume that Ralegh wrote "Give me my scallop-shell of quiet" while awaiting his execution, that George Boleyn's "O death, rock me asleep" has a similar starting point, or that Chidiock Tichbourne's "My prime of youth is but a frost of cares" relates to his execution as a Catholic martyr—I apologize for the monotony of the stimulus that real life provided in the sixteenth century—but none of these time-honored speculations impinge on the matter with which criticism is really concerned: the personality of the poet *qua* poet, the "personal signature he imposes on his work." Even when we have a fair body of work attached securely to the name of a known individual it does not follow that we have anything modern criticism can usefully deal with. The poems of Sir Arthur Gorges fill a fair-sized volume; but after reading through Miss Helen Sandison's impeccably edited pages one is still entitled to ask, "Who *is* Sir Arthur Gorges?" Certainly the task of assigning one other poem to Gorges on stylistic grounds would seem insuperably difficult. Gorges writes about his own life in a recognizable

way, and we can fill in the background of what he is saying
from historical sources. But, for all their documentation, his
poems are not suffused with Gorges's personality, are not
"Gorgian" in the way that others are "Sidneyan" or "Shelleyan" or "Drydenesque." He regards his role apparently as
that of the honest artificer, assimilating the actual event to the
traditional shape and the actual person to the traditional object.
Behind the screens of convention Gorges himself is invisible. I
take it that the essential point in all this is not that there are
difficulties in finding authors for all the poems in the period,
but that the poems so seldom profit from having known
authors.

It might be argued—and indeed it often is assumed—that
only bad poems suffer from this absence of personality. The
dispute between those who assume a gulf of mediocrity stretching between Wyatt and Sidney and those who defend the
interim is often conducted in terms that assume the essential
virtue of personality. The criticism of Yvor Winters and his
followers provides a good illustration of what I mean. Winters
is the founder of a modern movement asserting that the poetry
not only of Ralegh and Greville but also of Gascoigne, Googe,
Turberville, etc.—those that C. S. Lewis called "Drab"—is
superior to the poetry of Sidney and Spenser. This preference
is, of course, part of Winters's general admiration for poems
that seem to be descriptive of objective fact. When we read
"The Sixteenth Century Lyric in England," however, we discover that Winters's reasons for his high valuation of Ralegh
and Gascoigne are closely connected with his sense of their
personalities. His basic opposition is between "rhetoric" ("the
pleasures of rhetoric for its own sake") and what may be
briefly described as "honesty to experience." He is understandably reticent about using this phrase, but when he speaks ap-

provingly of "the laconic bitterness of Raleigh and the bitter terror of Nashe" or of "the moral grandeur, the grandeur of personal character to be discerned in Gascoigne and Raleigh" he is, if I understand him, asserting the value of states of mind he approves of, and assuming that these give the poems which express them their claim to value.

In this mode of valuation Winters is, of course, close to standard definitions of the lyric. We may take the definition from M. H. Abrams's handbook of literary terms: "The term [lyric] is used for any short poem presenting a single speaker (not necessarily the poet himself) who expresses a state of mind involving thought and feeling." The difficulty with this definition lies in the phrase "expresses a state of mind." Must this be confined to the meaning "gives us the sense of a man experiencing thought and feeling"? Must the lyric (that is, the good lyric) give us the sense of a speaker inside the poem?

To pursue this question we may glance at a poem which would not, I assume, meet Winters's requirements—it does not appear in Winters's own anthology or in John Williams's *English Renaissance Poetry*—but whose claim to be a major lyric poem of the period might be generally allowed: Sidney's double sestina, "Ye goat-herd gods that love the grassy mountains." Even its admirers must accept that this is a highly rhetorical poem which is highly self-conscious about its rhetoric, one in which we listen in vain for signs of the individual voice speaking out to express a state of mind. But these are not defects. Awareness of the rhetoric is in fact the key to the enjoyment of the poem, whose meaning is not expressed by its statements so much as enacted by its form, acquiring existence as the formal shape of the poem unrolls. What is more, there seem to be too many good poems of this kind in the period to allow the personal voice in the poem to be thought of as the

only value-conferring element. I do not wish to pursue the role
of music in the lyric poetry of the period; it raises more questions than it answers. But I should like to make a single point:
that music exercises a generalizing effect on the words of the
poem, moving the poetry away from any sense that it expresses
an individual's unique feelings. In so far as the age is one in
which "music and sweet poetry agree" it is one with a bias
toward generalized and impersonal lyric poetry.

Winters has attacked literary history (justifiably) for its
tendency to value individual poems as representative produc-
tions of "schools" of poetry. The attack (e.g., in his review of
C. S. Lewis's Oxford History of English Literature volume, in
*The Function of Criticism*) is perhaps excessively easy for him,
for he assumes that all good poems are basically the same—
objective descriptions from a morally approved point of view.
His "great tradition," derived from a single and repetitive criterion, is found in "the great poems of Gascoigne and Raleigh
and those most clearly resembling them by Greville, Jonson,
Donne and Shakespeare." Sidney and Spenser, on the other
hand, have "sensitivity to language . . . far in excess of their
moral intelligence"; they must not complicate our view of the
Renaissance lyric, for they are only (as John Williams tells us)
a "temporary displacement . . . an eccentric movement away
from the native tradition."

It would be easy to spend more space on Winters than on
the sixteenth-century lyric; but it is not my purpose to bandy
critical theories. In particular I do not wish to set against the
categories of the *Winterreise*—"plain versus eloquent," "native
versus Petrarchan"—some alternative system which preserves
the polarities and changes the values. This is what has happened in Winters's response to C. S. Lewis. Lewis's polarization
of "Drab" and "Golden" has found few defenders and Winters

strenuously objects to it. But though the objection is couched as a general opposition to the categories of literary history, the structure of Winters's own categories is identical; only the values have changed.

It is of course very difficult to present separate good poems and avoid any diagram of preference between them, unless one can avoid the issue by keeping to a narrow or doctrinaire sense of what "good" means. But let us begin by making an assumption that the sixteenth century offers different but equal kinds of lyric excellence—that (say) of the translation of Psalm CXXXIII in Byrd's *Songs of Sundry Natures* (1589):

> Behold how good a thing it is
> For brethren to agree,
> When men amongst them do no strife
> But peace and concord see.
> Full like unto the precious balm
> From Aaron's head that fell
> And did descend upon his beard
> His garment skirts until.
> And as the pleasant morning dew
> The mountains will relieve
> So God will bless where concord is
> And life eternal give.

and that (say) of the anonymous madrigal in Bateson's 1618 collection:

> Her hair the net of golden wire,
> Wherein my heart, led by my wandering eyes,
> So fast entangled is that in no wise
> It can nor will again retire;
> But rather will in that sweet bondage die
> Than break one hair to gain her liberty.

Naïvety and sophistication here face one another in such a way that they seem genuinely alternative virtues. Is it possible to speak of the Renaissance lyric so that both moods are given scope? The danger in literary history is its tendency to premature and unargued valuations. Clearly these poems are different one from another. Clearly each belongs to a large mass of poetry which reflects the qualities it possesses individually. On the whole it may be said that the style of the first belongs to the period from the sixties to the eighties, though various features of the style are found later; while the style of the second belongs to the nineties and the following decades. Literary history offers two obvious models for dealing with this situation: either one style develops into the other (A is less good than B) or one style is a decadent form of the other (B is less good than A). A careful reading through the work of the mid-century poets, Churchyard, Golding, Howells, Googe, Turberville, Gascoigne, Edwardes, Hunnis, suggests that neither of these models will serve to describe the relationship between the style of these poets—the style of the first poem above—and the style of the second poem, which is the style of Sidney, Lodge, and Daniel. I exclude Spenser from this distinction; in relation to it his position is highly ambiguous.

A careful reading suggests that neither style is a version of the other; each has as its aim a distinct image of the world, and other features are explicable in terms of this aim. What changes when poets move from one style to the other (if they move) is not only literary style but also the life-style of the persona who emerges from the body of their work.

From what was said earlier in this paper it might seem that I was now poised to advance to a distinction between the impersonal persona of a Gorges and the highly personal persona of a Sidney. I must confess to some intention of this kind; but in so bald a statement the distinction would seem to be neither useful nor true. Poetry in the "Golden" style of the second poem quoted is often as impersonal and conventional as any "Drab" poetry; Wyatt's songs might be thought of as both "Drab" and personal; and the poets of the mid-century are not to be described simply as men suspicious of versified egotism; their verse exhibits constantly the tension between the claims of erotic individualism and the larger claims of the society to which they belong.

It is important to note that the poets of the mid-century (I am thinking of Googe, Howell, Turberville, and Gascoigne) were the first English poets to publish collections of their own lyrics. It is not surprising that they did this in volumes bearing some marks of order and design. The idea of the auto-anthology is strange; but one can see it as forced on these poets by their social situation. Their choosing to publish cuts them off from the annals of the courtly lyric; but they were already cut off in the milieux of their lives and lyrics from Wyatt, Surrey, Vaux, Ralegh, Dyer, Oxford, Essex—the real courtly makers. The verse of Googe and his fellows is poorly designed for the private entertainment of great ladies and their companions. Their love songs, when compared to Wyatt's, lack the easy support of accepted background situations, and of the medieval traditions of court poem and court music. Wyatt can seem intensely personal and completely conventional at one and the same time. The mid-century poets have to be laboriously explicit in setting up a social background. The volumes seem to exist in order to create, in some sense, a cultured social world which the reader can join for the price of the book. The elaborate titles for their poems (described below) are obviously part of this intention to create explicitly what the court poets evoke and assume.

These authors have many things in common: they are scholars by courtesy of a Humanist education, translators from Latin and Italian, officials by profession (Inns-of-Court men predominantly), so that the world of their verse is cut off from their professional life in a way that is not true of the courtier. Their verses are a kind of *vers de société*. They are aimed at readers of known and accepted preferences and judgments, explicitly stated by the poet himself. The persona which dominates these poems is that of the moralist, living in a world of corruption. Again and again the authors return to the commonplaces of Contempt of the World:

What is this world, a net to snare the soul . . .

O Fortune false, how double are thy deeds . . .

Hope, whoso list, in life Hath but uncertain stay . . .

This is the basis of their sensibilities, the common ground against which their love poems have to make their effect. It follows that the love poetry of these men describes a social view of love, where the seeming individuality of each "I," each lover, is denied by the multiplication and monotony of Cupid's spoils:

Where fond affection bore the chiefest sway,
And where the blinded archer with his bow
Did glance at sundry gallants every day.

The technique of such poets can be seen as part of this effort to express a vision of reality. The poulter's measure and the fourteener are usually explained as reactions to late medieval metrical chaos; their extreme rigidity of rhythm in this view explains their vogue. But the rigidity of these meters may have a moral as well as a metrical aspect. It is not hard to imagine their attraction for the moralist who is stressing above all things the common lot that holds individual egotism in check. A highly sophisticated sensibility like Chapman's can give the fourteener a complex tread:

> Achilles' baneful wrath resound, O goddess, that imposed
> Infinite sorrows on the Greeks and many brave souls loosed
> From breasts heroic—sent them far, to that invisible cave
> That no light comforts.

But this is not what Howell and Turberville are aiming at. They aim not only at weight and solidity but also at effects of plainness. The persona they seek is that of a homespun philosopher, beloamed with proverbs and downright opinions, happy to echo the formulae that other men use and to depend on the same formulaic abstractions. Lewis, talking about the "Drab" style, says, in a moment of unusual dyslogistic candor: "If the poetry of the Drab Age was usually bad, that might be because new models induced minor talents to turn away from the thin, but real, trickle of poetry that still survived among the people." It is true that the Drab poets are not ballad-writers, on the whole: but it is important to notice they do not really turn away from the rustic. These poets may aim at the court in some sense (though I suspect that the adjective "courtly" is used much too freely and much too vaguely), but not in any sense that puts the court and the people in direct opposition. In a similar way, though we may call them men of learning, we should note that their learning is absorbed into a world where "Maro's learned quill" or "Senec's sappy sense" lie naturally cheek by jowl with the clodhopping integrity of country wisdom. This is not pastoral; indeed it is the opposite of pastoral, for it assumes that the tension between the images of court and country, on which pastoral depends, does not exist or should not exist.

The effort to project this same persona, to describe the same reality, probably explains vocabulary no less than meter. To modern ears their excess of Saxon monosyllables compounds the lumbering heaviness of meter, reinforced by alliteration. But pure or "clene" English has a status in this period and among this group that relates it to shooting with the bow, hawking and hunting, and keeping open house as our forefathers did. The distaste for inkhorn terms is not only and not primarily a literary response; it is part of patriotism. As Gascoigne remarks: "The most ancient English words are of one syllable, so that the more monosyllables that you use the truer Englishman you shall seem, and the less you shall smell of the inkhorn." The persona I have been speaking of is, among other features, self-consciously English.

The volumes of Gascoigne (*A Hundred Sundry Flowers*, 1573) and Turberville (*Epitaphs, Epigrams, Songs and Sonets*, 1567) are particularly interesting examples of the poetic stance I am describing. The two books are, in their structure, quite like one another. They are, in the main, collections of love poems strung along a thread of quasi-narrative. This does not mean that the social morality I have described as central to the mode is absent from them. They are pervaded by the shared scene of poetry-making, in which AB gives advice to CD and EF writes an answer on CD's behalf. The personal erotic emotion that these poets show us is always qualified by social judgment, either through straight moralization and return to the shared knowledge of human vanity, or by a kind of dramatization in which "the lover" is set in a social scene and so made available for our moral comments. This dramatization is a standard feature in collections of poetry from Tottel onwards. The elaborate titles which poems of this time are given provide a social context for the individual emotion:

> The lover being disdainfully abjected by a dame of high calling who had chosen (in his place) a plain fellow of baser condition, doth therefore determine to step aside, and before his departure giveth her this farewell in verse.

> The lover describeth his whole state unto his love and promising her his faithful good will assureth himself of her again.

I take it that these preparations for the poem are meant to guard us against assuming that the poet is addressing us directly with his own emotions or with those he thinks universal.

The most elaborate example of this dramatization of the egotism of the lover, and the separation of the poet's persona from the lover's, appears in Gascoigne's "The Adventures of Master F. J.," first printed in *A Hundred Sundry Flowers* and then (in a revised form) in *The Posies* (1575). The series of screens used to reveal this work to the public are worthy of Pope in number and complexity. Gascoigne's poems ("diverse discourses and verses invented upon sundry occasions by sundry gentlemen") are printed in *A Hundred Sundry Flowers*, we are told, only because G. T. passed them to H. W. who gave them to A. B., a printer. In "F. J." the situation is even more complex. Here we have the story of F. J.'s adventures told in the third person by G. T. who disclaims any more knowledge of them than what F. J. once told him; the sole ostensible purpose in telling the story is to explain how F. J. came to write the poems ("having taken in hand only to copy out his verses"): "Well, I dwell too long upon these particular points in discoursing this trifling history, but that the same is

the more apt mean of introduction to the verses which I mean
to rehearse unto you."

The poems themselves are thus continually hedged about
with explanations designed to infringe their independent status.
And it is not only the tale that continually thrusts itself between the poems and the reader; but G. T., as he tells us what
led up to and what resulted from the poems, also cocoons them
in literary criticism:

> This ballad or howsoever I shall term it percase you will
> not like and yet in my judgment it hath great good store of
> deep invention, and for the order of the verse it is not com-
> mon; I have not heard many of like proportion. Some will
> account it but a diddledom, but whoso had heard F. J. sing it
> to the lute by a note of his own device I suppose he would
> esteem it to be a pleasant diddledom, and for my part, if I
> were not partial, I would say more in commendation of it
> than now I mean to do, leaving it to your and like judgments.

Reading the poems one can see why Gascoigne wishes to
dramatize the context so fully. Like those of other Drab poets
Gascoigne's lyrics are remarkably bare of any ambiguity in the
attitude of the "I" speaking or indeed of any effective inner
symbolism. Like the prose of "F. J." they present, on the
whole, straightforward reactions to a believable social scene:

> After he grew more bold and better acquainted with his
> Mistress' dispositions he adventured one Friday in the morn-
> ing to go into her chamber, and thereupon wrote as follow-
> eth, which he termed a Friday's breakfast:

> G. T.

> That selfsame day, and of that day the hour
> When she does reign that mocked Vulcan the smith
> And thought it meet to harbour in her bower

Some gallant guest for her to dally with—
That blessed hour, that blest and happy day
I thought it meet with hasty steps to go
Unto the lodge wherein my lady lay
To laugh for joy or else to weep for woe.
And lo, my lady, of her wonted grace,
First lent her lips to me (as for a kiss)
And after that her body to embrace
Wherein Dame Nature wrought no thing amiss.
What followed next guess you that know the trade,
For in this sort my Friday's feast I made.

                                                            F. J.

The words here mean just what they say, and no more. The Ovidian model for the poem (*Amores* I.v) is very simple; but the witty style of Ovid keeps a balance between reality and dream. Gascoigne's combination of realism and simplicity makes it impossible for the "I" in the poem to express any balance of alternative attitudes. Gascoigne achieves something like balance by telling us in the prose links both what F.J. felt and what came (and indeed was bound to come) of his adventure. Even when Gascoigne borrows the furniture of psychological symbolism from Petrarch, as in the third poem:

Love, hope and death do stir in me such strife
As never man but I led such a life,

the symbolism is not left as a sufficient description of F. J.'s mind; it is isolated and contained as a merely literary device by G. T.'s comment: "I have heard F. J. say that he borrowed the invention of an Italian. But were it a translation or invention (if I be judge) it is both pretty and pithy."

There *is* symbolism in "F. J."—dreams, games, inserted tales, significant names, significant attire—but these are all presented as part of a social mode, being manipulated by sophisticated but real people. The creation of a world possessed by its symbols, and so cut off from "real" life, has to wait for the *Arcadia* (c.1580) and, more effectively, *Astrophil and Stella* (c.1582). This does not imply, of course, a general advance. There is often a vacuity about symbolism which exists for its own sake, cut off from the controlling sense of "real" life—as in much nineties pastoral. But perhaps the independence of the individual lyric depends on the poet being willing to take the risk of such vacuity.

A comparison between "F. J." and Sidney's *Arcadia* might well be thought unfair; and in several respects the works are too unlike to be secure bases for a general comparison of the seventies and the nineties. It is obvious, however, that there is a larger shift in rhetoric at this time which accommodates the difference between these two works and much else. To be curt, the basis of rhetoric moves from schemes to tropes, from figures of words to figures of thought. Anaphora, alliteration, repetition, and cumulation of various kinds give way to puns, paradoxes, and shifts of tone through imagery. If we look back at the Gascoigne poem "That selfsame day . . ." quoted above we will notice not only the lack of image and symbol (discussed already) but also the positive effect of the repetitions in carrying the impetus through to the end of the octave. The sense of order in the poem is achieved by the balancing of its various effects of movement into a final repose; and these movements are across the surface of a clearly defined reality. We may compare with this the first poem in the *Arcadia:*

Transformed in show, but more transformed in mind,
I cease to strive, with double conquest foiled;
For, woe is me, my powers all I find
With outward force and inward treason spoiled.

For from without came to mine eyes the blow
Whereto mine inward thoughts did faintly yield;
Both these conspired poor Reason's overthrow;
False in myself thus have I lost the field.
Thus are my eyes still captive to one sight;
Thus all my thoughts are slaves to one thought still;
Thus reason to his servants yields his right;
Thus is my power transformed to your will.
    What marvel then I take a woman's hue,
    Since what I see, think, know is all but you?

This is what Pyrocles sings when discovered dressed as the
Amazon Zelmane. The situation that the poem crystallizes is
more symbolic than narrative and the technique reflects this
environment. The "story" the poem has to tell—"I have been
transformed"—is merely a theme, which is worked through the
contrast of inner and outer to yield a series of interlinked variations. Once again the sense of order in the poem can be attrib-
uted to its balancing the various effects; but these no longer
concern physical movement, but rather the drift of transformation in the images. The poem moves from outward femininity
to inward effeminacy, from the confession of powerlessness to
an analysis of the process involved: from blow to submission,
to treason to self-defeat; and beyond defeat to the captivity
which eventually returns to the "power" of the opening and
locates it afresh in the unprepared-for "you." The sonnet thus
ends with a confession of passion which continues the argument of the poem, but reverses the emotion (shame) with
which it began. The language here, unlike that of the Gascoigne poem, is never literal. These things, the "blow," the
"yielding," the "conspiring," never really happened; they measure the potentials in the human mind; and it is with the balance of potentials that the whole poem is concerned—indeed it

is with the balance of potentials that the whole career of Pyrocles-Zelmane is concerned. By this I do not mean that the *Arcadia* is not an explicitly moral work; its whole world is eventually submitted to a formal moral judgment. But the morality of the individual part and of the individual poem is largely self-contained. The integral poems of the *Arcadia* reflect, of course, the situations of the persons who sing them; but they exist, the poems and the situations, in parallel rather than sequence, as parallel self-explanatory emblems. The whole work, indeed, may be seen as a collection of these emblems rather than a straightforward narrative. In these terms it is easy to see the relationship between the *Arcadia* and the *Astrophil and Stella*. The sonnet sequence is likewise a collection of parallel emblems. The "story" has shrunk still further; and was to go on shrinking throughout the remaining lifetime of the Renaissance lyric. The individual lyric has absorbed into itself the moral "placing" of its own material. The lyric for the reader (to this extent unlike the lyric for fellow courtiers of Wyatt) has acquired a mode which enables it to dispense with the prose link or the planned sequence, or even the circle of named (or initialed) friends; and in this more public form, freed from its dependence on court music and the medieval song-tradition, it has returned to something of the power and sophistication of Wyatt's songs.

In *Astrophil and Stella* this new mode is dominated by the brilliance of the personality it reveals. The opposition that is set up between the self-justifying ego and the traditional formulas—"Let dainty wits cry on the sisters nine," "You that do search for every purling spring"—might suggest that these give the essential terms for a separation of this new poetry from the old. But a survey of "Golden" poetry in general suggests that the essential element is not personality but the aesthetic autonomy that this poetry creates for its readers. It is this that seems to account for its losses as well as its profits, its failures as well as its successes. For if the poorer "Drab" lyric seeking weight achieves only ponderous obviousness, so the lyric which aims to create an autonomous world of delight often concocts only an irrelevant one, achieving not elegant ease but vacuous sophistication.

HELEN VENDLER

# The Re-invented Poem:

## GEORGE HERBERT'S ALTERNATIVES

ONE of the particular virtues of Herbert's poetry is its extremely provisional quality. His poems are ready at any moment to change direction or to modify attitudes. Even between the title and the first line, Herbert may rethink his position. There are lines in which the nominal experiences or subjects have suffered a sea-change, so that the poem we think we are reading turns into something quite other. The more extreme cases occur, of course, in Herbert's "surprise endings," what Valentina Poggi calls his "final twist,"[1] where, as Arnold Stein says, Herbert "dismisses the structure, issues, and method" of the entire poem, "rejecting the established terms" on which the poem has been constructed, as he does in "Clasping of Hands," which ends, after playing for nineteen lines on the notions of "thine" and "mine," with the exclamation, "Or rather make no Thine and Mine!"[2] In cases less abrupt, Her-

[1] Valentina Poggi, *George Herbert* (Bologna, 1967), pp. 203 ff.
[2] Arnold Stein, *George Herbert's Lyrics* (Baltimore, 1968), pp. 150, 151.

bert's fluid music lulls our questions: we scarcely see his oddities, or if we see them, they cease to seem odd, robed as they are in the seamless garment of his cadence. When in "Vertue," he breathes, "Sweet rose," we echo, "sweet rose," and never stop to think that nothing in the description he gives us of the rose—that it is angry in hue, that it pricks the eye of the rash beholder, that its root is ever in the grave—bears out the epithet "sweet." Is the stanza about a sweet rose, as the epithet would have us believe, or about a bitter rose? This is a minor example of Herbert's immediate critique of his own clichés ("The Collar" may serve us as a major example) and poses, in little, the problem of this essay: how can we give an accurate description of Herbert's constantly self-critical poems, which so often reject premises as soon as they are established?

Herbert's willingness to abolish his primary terms of reference or his primary emotion at the last possible moment speaks for his continually provisional conduct of the poem. After begging, for twenty lines, for God's grace to drop from above, Herbert suddenly reflects that there is, after all, another solution, equally good: if God will not descend to him, he may be brought to ascend to God:

> O come! for thou dost know the way:
> Or if to me thou wilt not move,
> Remove me, where I need not say,
>     *Drop from above.*                              ("Grace")

In part, this is simply the cleverness of finding a way out of a dilemma; but more truly, in Herbert's case, the ever-present alternative springs from his conviction that God's ways are not his ways—"I cannot skill of these thy wayes." If man insists on one way—that his God, for instance, drop grace on him—it is almost self-evident that God may have a different way in store to grant the request, and Herbert bends his mind to imagining what it might be—in this case, that God, instead of moving himself, should *remove* Herbert. The pun in the "solution" shows verbally the pairing of alternatives to accomplish the same object. Precision is all, and when Herbert catches himself in careless speech, he turns on himself with a vengeance. In "Giddinesse," human beings are reproved for fickleness, and God is asked, first, to "mend" us; but no, we are beyond mending, and so Herbert must ask God to "make" us anew; but no, one creation will not suffice—God will have to "re-make" us daily, since we sin daily:

> Lord, *mend*
> or rather *make* us; one creation/ Will not suffice our turn;
> Except thou *make us dayly*, we shall spurn
>     Our own salvation.

Equally, when Herbert finds himself lapsing into frigid pulpit oratory, he pulls himself up sharply from his clichés about "Man" and in the last breath turns inward, "My God, I mean myself." These second thoughts are everywhere in Herbert. The wanton lover, he says, can expend himself ceaselessly in praising his beloved; why does not the poet do the same for God? "Lord, cleare thy gift," he asks in "Dulnesse," "that with a constant wit/ I may—" May what? we ask, and if we continue the analogy we would say, "That I may love and praise thee as lovers their mistresses." Something like this must have passed through Herbert's mind, and have been rejected as overweening, so that instead he writes:

> Lord, cleare thy gift, that with a constant wit
>     I may but look towards thee:
> *Look* only; for to *love* thee, who can be,
>     What angel fit?

The italics on "look" and "love" show Herbert, as it were, doing the revision of his poem in public, substituting the tentative alternative for the complacent one. He takes into account our expectation, prompted by his analogy with lovers, of the word "love," and rebukes himself and us for daring to ask such a divine gift. The proper reading of the poem must realize both the silent expectation and the rebuke, as Herbert changes his mind at the last moment.

Some of Herbert's most marked and beautiful effects come from this constant re-invention of his way. One of the most spectacular of these occurs in "A True Hymne": Herbert has been praising the faithful heart over the instructed wit, and says:

> The fineness which a hymne or psalme affords,
> Is, when the soul unto the lines accords.
>
> . . . If th'heart be moved,
> Although the verse be somewhat scant,
>     God doth supply the want.

He then gives us an example of God's supplying the want:

> As, when th'heart sayes (sighing to be approved)
> O, could I love! and stops: God writeth—

Logically, what God should write to reassure the soul, is *Thou dost love*. To wish to love is to love; but to love God, Herbert bethinks himself, is first to have been loved by God (as he tells us in the first "Affliction") and so God, instead of ratifying the soul's wish, *O could I love!* by changing it from the optative to the declarative, changes instead the soul from subject to

object, and writes *Loved*. If we do not intuit, as in "Dulnesse,"
the "logical" ending *Thou dost love,* we cannot see how Herbert has refused a banal logic in favor of a truer metaphysical
illogic, conceived of at the last possible utterance of the poem.
He stops in his course, veers round, writes *Loved,* and ends the
poem in what is at once a better pride and a better humility.

What does this mean about Herbert's mind, this rethinking
of the poem at every moment? It means that he allows his
moods free play and knows that logic is fallible: one may want
one thing today and quite another on the Last Day, for instance. When Herbert is tormented in turn by the jeering of
worldly Beauty, Money, Glory, and Wit, he remains silent, but
says in his heart that on the Last Day he will be revenged,
when his God will answer his tormentors for him: "But thou
shalt answer, Lord, for me." And yet, as soon as he truly thinks
of that scene on the Last Day, he re-invents it: the last stanza
of "The Quip" shows Herbert's God, not vindicating at large
the now-triumphant soul, not administering an anathema to the
defeated worldly glories, but engaging in an almost silent
colloquy alone with the faithful soul:

> Yet when the houre of thy designe
> To answer these fine things shall come;
> Speak not at large; say, I am thine:
> And then they have their answer home.

When we hear, in "Love Unknown," of God's wishes for Herbert (which of course amount to Herbert's best wishes for
himself) we learn that "Each day, each houre, each moment of
the week,/ [He] fain would have [him] be new, tender,
quick." Nothing is to be taken for granted, nothing should be
habitual, nothing should be predictable: every day, every hour,

every moment things have to be thought through again, and the surface of the heart must be renewed, quickened, mended, suppled.

An accurate description of Herbert's work implies a recognition of where his true originality lies. A few years ago this was the subject of some debate between William Empson and Rosemond Tuve, when Empson claimed as "original" images which Miss Tuve proved traditional in iconographic usage. Empson retorted that traditional images could nevertheless bear a significant unconscious meaning, and that choice of image in itself was indicative, a statement which deserves more attention. The attic of "tradition" is plundered differently by different poets, and each poet decides what décor he will choose from the Christian storehouse in order to deck his stanzas. Though every single image in a poem may be "traditional," the choice of emphasis and exclusion is individual and revealing. Herbert, of course, often begins poems with, or bases poems upon, a traditional image or scene or prayer or liturgical act or biblical quotation; and our knowledge of these bases has been deepened by Miss Tuve's book. But a question crying out to be answered is what he makes of the traditional base. A similar question would ask what he does with the experiential *donnée*, personal rather than "traditional," of an autobiographical poem. In short, what are some of Herbert's characteristic ways of "conducting" a poem? My answer, in general, appears in my title, and in the examples I have so far offered: Herbert "re-invents" the poem afresh as he goes along; he is constantly criticizing what he has already written down, and finding the original conception inadequate, whether the original conception be the Church's, the Bible's, or his own. Nothing is exempt from his critical eye, when he is at his best, and there is almost no cliché of religious expression or personal experience that he does not reject after being tempted into expressing it. A poem by Herbert is often "written" three times over, with several different, successive, and self-contradictory versions co-existing. A different sort of poet would have written one version, have felt dissatisfied with the truth or accuracy of the account, would then have written a second, more satisfactory version, have rethought that stage, and have produced at last a "truthful" poem. Herbert prefers to let his successive "re-thinkings" and re-inventions follow one another, but without warning us of the discrepancies among his several accounts, just as he followed his original qualification of the rose as sweet with a long description of the rose as bitter, without any of the usual "buts" or "yets" of semantic contradiction. (I should add that the evidence we have in the Williams manuscript, which gives Herbert's revisions of some poems, supports these conjectures on Herbert's rethinking of his lines, but what I wish to emphasize is not his revisions before he reached a final version but rather the re-invention of the poem as it unfolds itself.)

The rest of this essay will be concerned with larger examples of Herbert's re-inventing of different sorts; and I begin with a combination of the liturgical, the ethical, and the biblical, in the poem called "The Invitation." In this poem, Herbert the priest is inviting sinners to the sacraments. He is probably remembering, in the beginning, St. Paul's statement (in Romans 14:21) that it is good neither to eat flesh nor to drink wine, and he begins his invitation with the Pauline view of sinners as prodigal gluttons and winebibbers, whose taste is their waste, and who are defined by wine:

> Come ye hither All, whose taste
>     Is your waste;

Save your cost, and mend your fare.
    . . .

Come ye hither All, whom wine
    Doth define,
Naming you not to your good.

For Herbert, though, St. Paul's revulsion is not congenial; Herbert, who "knows the ways of pleasure" and knows as well the pains of remorse, begins to alter his portrait of swinish and sensual sinners in a remarkable way. In the third stanza, the sinners become "All, whom pain/ Doth arraigne"; in the fourth stanza they are people who are misled by their delight to graze outside their bounds; and by the astonishing fifth stanza the sinners are positively seraphic:

Come ye hither All, whose love
    Is your dove,
And exalts you to the skie:
Here is love, which having breath
    Ev'n in death,
After death can never die.

Sinners, in fact, are finally seen in the poem as people with all the right instincts—they want joy, delight, exaltation, and love; and that, Herbert implies, is what the redeemed want too. The sinners, misled in their desires, seek the carnal and the temporary, Venus' doves instead of the Holy Spirit, sky instead of heaven. The equation of wants in saints and sinners permits Herbert's final startling stanza:

Lord, I have invited all . . .
For it seems but just and right
    In my sight,
Where is All, there All should be.

The liturgical "dignum et justum est" and the verbally indistinguishable "All's" (both capitalized) give the sinners a
final redeemed and almost divine place at the banquet. The
poem amounts, though implicitly, to a total critique of the
usual scorn toward sinners, a scorn which Herbert himself began with, but which in the course of the poem he silently rejects. He makes no announcement of his rejection as he changes
his view, and therefore we are likely to miss it, as we miss
other changes of mind in his poems. Nevertheless, over and
over, Herbert re-invents what he has received and embraced,
correcting it to suit his own corrected notions of reality.[3]

Our received notion of Doomsday, for instance, is a severe
one, the Dies Irae when the whole world, as Herbert says
elsewhere, will turn to coal. That day is sometimes thought of
from God's point of view, as when we say, "He shall come to
judge the living and the dead," or from the human point of
view (as when St. Paul says, "We shall be changed, be raised
incorruptible"), but Herbert chooses to think of it via the
fanciful construct of the emotions felt by the bodies already-
dead-but-not-yet-raised, unhappy in their posthumous insensi-
bility, imprisonment, noisomeness, fragmentation, and decay.
The "fancy" behind the poem is that it is not so much God
who awaits the Last Day, nor is it those on earth who wish to

[3] When John Wesley rewrote "The Invitation" for hymn-singing,
he did far more than adapt the meter. (An adaptation faithful to
Herbert's meaning had been made in 1697, reprinted now in Select
Hymns Taken out of Mr. Herbert's Temple [1697], Augustan Reprint Society No. 98 [Los Angeles, 1962], pp. 31–32). Wesley's
adaptation insists on the wickedness and carnality of the sinners,
intensifying in every case Herbert's description, and showing none
of Herbert's changes of attitude. Wesley's version may be found in
the Collected Poetical Works of John and Charles Wesley, ed. G.
Osborn (London, 1868–69) I, 111–13.

put on immortality, nor is it the disembodied souls in heaven, but
rather it is those poor soulless corrupting bodies confined in
their graves. It is they who really yearn after a lively and
sociable Judgment Day, when they can each "jog the other,
each one whispring, *Live you, brother?*" A poem like this
begins with a poet thinking not "What are the traditions
about Doomsday?" but rather, "I know what is usually said
about Doomsday, but what would it really be like, and who
really longs for it?" Herbert's poem is very different from
Donne's more conventional "At the round earth's imagined
corners, blow/ Your trumpets, Angels, and arise, arise/ From
death, you numberless infinities/ Of souls," a poem in which
we at once recognize the Doomsday conventions at work.

Herbert's corrections extend, of course, to himself as well as
to his liturgical or biblical sources, and these self-corrections
are his most interesting re-inventions. Some of them do not at
first sight seem personal, and since these are rather deceptive,
I should like to begin with one of them—his self-correction in
the sonnet "Prayer." This famous poem is impersonally
phrased, and is, as everyone knows, a definition poem consisting of a chain of metaphors describing prayer. "Rethinking" is
in fact most likely to occur in ordinary life in just this sort of
definition-attempt, but whereas in life this rethinking and re-
fining is generally an exercise in intellectual precision, in
Herbert it is an exercise in the affections. Herbert's images
cannot be said to be ambiguous; they are, though sometimes
recondite, in general perfectly clear. It is the whole which is
complex, a something (prayer, in this instance) which can
be any number of things, not only at different times, but even
at once. This tolerance of several notions at once appeals to
us in Herbert nowadays, just as his profusion of images
appeals. As Rosemond Tuve pointed out in *Elizabethan and*

*Metaphysical Imagery,* an attempt to make clear the logical actions or passions of a subject will all by itself engender images, as it does in "Prayer." These twenty-six or so images of prayer tell us several things. To begin with the easiest, we know the sort of prayer which is an engine against the Almighty, which reverses the Jovian thunderbolt and hurls it back at its source. It is not too much to call this the prayer of resentment uttered by the wounded soul; it is the sinner's tower (with overtones of Babel) raised against a seemingly unjust God. We have any number of these "rebellious" prayers in the Herbert canon. To pray in this indignant warlike way is scarcely a sign of perfection; it is an emanation of the lowest possible state above the outright rebellion of sin. The next easiest group of images in the poem, by all odds, is the group toward the end—the Milkie Way, the Bird of Paradise, the Land of Spices. When prayer seems like this to the soul, the soul is clearly experiencing an unearthly level of feeling quite without aggressive elements. The poem, then, arrives at this state of joy from an earlier state of anger and rebellion; so much is clear as soon as we assume a single consciousness behind the metaphors of the poem. But what, then, are we to make of the beginning of the poem, which seems neither aggressive nor exalted?

> Prayer, the Churches banquet, Angels age,
>> God's breath in man returning to his birth,
>> The soul in paraphrase, heart in pilgrimage,
> The Christian plummet sounding heav'n and earth.

In what state is the soul when it speaks these lines? It must be a state which precedes the sudden rise of injured "virtue" in the use of engines and thunderbolts and spears against God; it is certainly not the heavenly state of the sestet. These lines which begin the sonnet are, in fact, without affect; they are the lines of the man who sets himself to pray frigidly, out of duty, drawing his metaphors not from feeling but from doctrine. What has he been taught, theologically, in dogma, about prayer? That it is the banquet of the church, that angels determine their age by how long they have been praying, that it engages both the heart and the soul, that it is "the Christian plummet" connecting the church militant to the church triumphant. When, from these artificialities, the speaker turns to his own feelings and takes stock of his own state and lapses into his own resentment, the poem takes on human reality: what, thinks Herbert, aside from these stock phrases, is prayer really? to me? now? A weapon, a spear, against the God who cripples my projects and cross-biasses me; and the aggressive images multiply. But that weapon (in the traditional image on which the entire poem hinges), by piercing Christ's side, initiates a countermovement, not of Jovian thunder this time but of grace, an infusion transforming the workaday world into the Sabbath (or rather, a transposing not a transforming, says Herbert with his usual precision; we are not changed but glorified). Whereas earlier the man praying had been active, launching engines, building towers, piercing with spears, he now relaxes in an ecstasy of passivity; prayer becomes a constellation of experienced essences, "softness and peace and joy and love and bliss." But Herbert cannot rest in that passivity of sensation; with a remarkable energy he introduces, again just as the poem is about to end in its celestial geography, the hitherto neglected intellect. Prayer, he says, correcting his delighted repose, is in the last analysis not simply a *datum*, something given, but a *comprehensum*, something understood. This phrase is at once the least and the most explicit in the

poem. Finally the poet understands, and is no longer the frigid
reciter of theological clichés, the resentful beggar, the aggressive hurler of thunderbolts, the grateful receiver of Manna,
nor the seeker of a Land of Spices. As a final definition, "something understood" abolishes or expunges the need for explana-
tory metaphors. Metaphor, Herbert seems to say, is after all
only an approximation; once something is understood, we can
fall silent; once the successive rethinkings of the definition have
been made, and the truth has been arrived at, the poem is over.

To arrive at that truth, to be able to end the poem, is often
difficult. "The Temper" (I) has to try three different endings
before it succeeds in ending itself satisfactorily, or at least to
Herbert's satisfaction. He has complained that God is stretching him too hard, subjecting him to exaltations succeeded by
depressions:

> O rack me not to such a vast extent!
> Those distances belong to thee.

God's stretching and then contracting him suggests to Herbert
another image, not this time the rack but another image of
equal tension, introduced with a characteristic concessive
"yet"—

> Yet take thy way; for sure thy way is best:
> Stretch or contract me, thy poore debter:
> This is but tuning of my breast,
> To make the musick better.

If Herbert had been content (as he sometimes could be) with
resolution on an easy level, there it was. Herbert's pain does
not diminish, but he has found a new vision of God to explain

it by: God is no longer the inquisitor torturing his victim on the rack; he is rather the temperer, the tuner of Herbert's heartstrings. The ending is adequate enough, and in fact Herbert's unknown adapter of 1697 stopped here, deleting Herbert's final stanza: to him the poem was finished, since Herbert had rediscovered the true "corrective" meaning of suffering.[4] But for Herbert the poem was not finished. The image of tuning still adhered to the poem's original primitive and anthropocentric notion of being stretched, of being first lifted by God to heaven and then dashed to earth. From a more celestial point of view, of course, heaven and earth are equally in God's presence and of his making, so Herbert repents of his shortsightedness, and invents a brilliant coda to his poem, expunging all its former terms of spatial reference:

> Whether I flie with angels, fall with dust,
>   Thy hands made both, and I am there.

The compact use of the one adverb—"there"—to stand for two places, heaven and earth, because both were made by God's hands, seems yet another final resolution of the distances in the poem. Still, Herbert is not satisfied. He continues with what seems at first to be a reiteration; we expect him to say that God's power makes everywhere, heaven and earth alike, one place. Instead, he says the reverse:

> Thy power and love, my love and trust,
>   Make one place everywhere.

In short, Herbert first rewrote racking as tuning, then he rewrote distance as unity ("there"), and then he rewrote unity

---

[4] *Select Hymns,* p. 13.

("one place") as immensity ("everywhere"). We should not forget that he was rewriting at the same time the cause of this transformation: at first everything was his God's doing, but at the penultimate line the change becomes a cooperative act in which two loves intersect, and God's power is conjoined with man's trust.

In addition to correcting himself, whether in the impersonal terms of "Prayer" or in the terms of repeated experience in "The Temper," Herbert corrects his autobiography, as usual not flaunting his re-inventions. They are for us usually the discoveries of a second reading, since at first we take them wholly for granted. The blandness of most critical paraphrase of Herbert indicates that readers have been misled by the perfect grace of the finished poem, and have concluded that an uninterrupted cadence means an uninterrupted ripple of thought. Herbert knew better: he said his thoughts were all a case of knives. The wounds of those knives are clearest in the autobiographical poems, those three great statements—"Affliction" (I), "The Flower," and "The Forerunners." In "The Forerunners," the simplest of the three, Herbert complains that in age he is losing his poetic powers, and he offers several alternative explanations of the loss, which a more anxious poet would be at pains to reconcile with each other. Herbert simply lets them stand; truth, not coherence, is his object. First, the harbingers of age come and evict his "sparkling notions," who are of course guiltless since they are forcibly "disparked." They and Herbert suffer together. Next it seems as though the "sweet phrases, lovely metaphors," are not being evicted but are leaving of their own free will; echoing Wyatt, Herbert asks reproachfully, "But will ye leave me thus?" accusing them of ingratitude after all his care of them. Next, they are no longer ungrateful children leaving home but rather

fully of age, seduced virgins: "Has some fond lover tic'd thee
to thy bane?" Finally, they are debased, willingly prostituting
themselves in the service of the lover who loves dung, and, in
Herbert's last bitterness, even their essence and power are denied them. They are no longer creative "enchanting" forces
but only "embellishments" of meaning. There is no resolution
to these successive metaphors of loss—no comprehensive view
is taken at the end, and we suffer with Herbert the final pre-
tended repudiation of those servants who have in fact deserted
him. His powerful love of his "beauteous words" has its own
independent force within the poem, but so does his gloomy
denial of value to those words at the end. The only true critical description of poems such as this must be a successive
one; a global description is bound to be misleading.

"Affliction" (I) is too long a poem to be taken up in detail
here, but it, like "The Forerunners," depends on a series of
inconsistent metaphors for a single phenomenon, God's treat-
ment of his creature. Herbert's ingenuity is matched only by
his frankness. His God is at first a seducer, "enticing" Herbert's heart; next he is a sovereign distributing "gracious bene-
fits," then an enchanter "bewitching" Herbert into his family;
he is an honest wage-paying master; he is a king dispensing
hope of high pleasure; he is a mother, indulgent:

> At first thou gav'st me milk and sweetnesses;
>   I had my wish and way.

But then God becomes one who inflicts sickness, and the poet
groans with the psalmist, "Sicknesses cleave my bones." Worse,
God becomes a murderer—"Thou took'st away my life"—
and an unfair murderer at that, leaving his creature with no
means of suitably vengeful retaliation—"A blunted knife/ Was

of more use than I." God sends famine, and Herbert becomes one of Pharaoh's lean kine: "Thus thinne and lean without a fence or friend,/ I was blown through with ev'ry storm and winde." In two lines of sinister genius, God is said to "betray" Herbert to paralysis (a "lingring" book) and death (he "wraps" Herbert in an unmistakably shroudlike gown). Next, God becomes a physician, deluding Herbert with his "sweetned pill," but then cruelly undoing his own healing, he "throws" Herbert into more sicknesses. God's last action seems his wickedest, surpassing all his previous enticements and tortures; he "clean forgets" his poet, and the abandonment is worse than the attention. These indictments of God are only one strain in this complaint, with its personal hesitations, accusations, self-justifications, and remorse, but they show Herbert's care and accuracy in describing his own notions of God as they changed from episode to episode. There is a remarkable lack of censorship; even with the Psalms as precedent, Herbert shows his absolute willingness to say how things were, to choose the accurate verb, to follow the truth of feeling. We can only guess at Herbert's inconsistencies of self-esteem which underlie the inconsistencies in this portrait of God. This God, changeable as the skies, first lightning then love and then lightning again, is reflected from a self first proud then craven and then proud again, a self which does not know whether it is a child or a victim or a dupe, a self for whom all self-assertion provoked a backwash of guilt.

With that guilt came a sense of God's absence, and that experience, habitual with Herbert, is the central topic of the third of these autobiographical poems, "The Flower." Just as the sonnet "Prayer" had redefined, over and over, with increasing approximation to the truth, what prayer is, so "The Flower" redefines, over and over, with increasing approximation to the truth, what has in fact been happening to Herbert. We are told that he has suffered a period of God's disfavor, during which he drooped, but that God has now returned to him and so he flourishes once again. This simple two-stage event could have been told, presumably, in a simple chronological account; but no, we are given several versions of the experience undergone. It is this repetitiveness, incidentally, here and elsewhere in Herbert, which caused George Herbert Palmer to class this poem together with others as redundant, lacking that fineness of structure he saw in Herbert's simpler two-part and three-part poems.[5] The redundancy is apparent, but not real; each time the experience is redescribed, it is altered, and each retelling is a critique of the one before.

The first version of Herbert's experience is a syntactically impersonal one, told without the "I": Herbert could be meditating on some universally known phenomenon:

> How fresh, O Lord, how sweet and clean
> Are thy returns! ev'n as the flowers in spring;
>    To which, besides their own demean,
> The late-past frosts tributes of pleasure bring.
>      Grief melts away
>      Like snow in May
>    As if there were no such cold thing.

Now these last three lines say something not strictly true. We do keep a memory of grief. But in the first flush of reconciliation, Herbert generously says that God has obliterated all past grief in the soul. This version of the incident also says that God has been absent and has now returned, just as spring

<hr>

[5] George Herbert Palmer, ed., *The Works of George Herbert* (Boston, 1905), I, 144.

absents itself and then returns, in a natural cyclical process.
We, and Herbert, shall discover in the course of the poem
how untrue these statements, about the cyclical absence of
God and the obliteration of grief, are.

The second stanza gives us yet another, and almost equally
rosy, view of Herbert's experience, this time in the first person:

>     Who would have thought my shrivel'd heart
> Could have recover'd greennesse? It was gone
>     Quite under ground; as flowers depart
> To see their mother-root, when they have blown;
>         Where they together,
>         All the hard weather
> Dead to the world, keep house unknown.

Here the period of grief is represented as, after all, not so
difficult; it was not God who went away, really, but rather
Herbert; and his absence was on the whole cosy, like the winter
hibernation of bulbs, where the flowers, in comfortable
company, visiting their mother the root, keep house together
with her, while the weather is harsh aboveground. This certainly
does not sound like a description of grief, but like a
situation of sociable comfort; the only ominous word here,
keeping us in touch with the truth, is "shrivel'd," which sorts
very ill with the familial underground housekeeping.

So far, a cloak of palliation lies over the truth. But when
Herbert has to summarize what this experience of grief followed
by joy has taught him, he admits that he finds the God
who lies behind such alternations of emotion an arbitrary and
incomprehensible one, who one day kills (a far cry from absenting
himself) and another day quickens, all by a word, an

absolute fiat. We are helpless to predict God's actions or to describe his intent; we await, defenseless, his unintelligible decisions, his arbitrary power:

> These are thy wonders, Lord of power,
> Killing and quickning, bringing down to hell
>     And up to heaven in an houre;
> Making a chiming of a passing-bell.
>             We say amisse,
>             This or that is:
> Thy word is all, if we could spell.

An early anthologist of Herbert cut off the poem here;[6] for him, and we may suspect for George Herbert Palmer, too, the poem might just as well have ended with this summarizing stanza. For Herbert, it could not; he has presented us with too many contradictions. Does God absent himself cyclically, like the spring, or arbitrarily and unpredictably? Is God only benevolent, or in fact a malevolent killer as well? Was it he that was absent, or Herbert? Was the period of absence one of hellish grief or one of sociable retirement? The poem had begun in earthly joy, but now, with the admission that we cannot spell and that God's word is arbitrary and incomprehensible, Herbert's resentment of his earthly condition has gained the ascendancy, and he repudiates wholly the endless emotional cycles of mortal life:

> O that I once past changing were,
> Fast in thy Paradise, where no flower can wither!

[6] James Montgomery, *The Christian Poet* (Glasgow, 1827), pp. 243–44.

Not God's changeableness, but his own, is now the issue; the
"withering" and "shriveling" are now uppermost in his mind,
as his past grief, tenacious in memory and not at all melted
away, comes once again to his mind.

Yet once more, for the fourth time, he recapitulates his experience. This time he does it in the habitual mode, the present tense of habit, emphasizing its deadly repetitiveness:

> Many a spring I shoot up fair,
> Offring at heav'n, growing and groning thither. . . .

> But while I grow in a straight line,
> Still upwards bent, as if heav'n were mine own,
>     Thy anger comes, and I decline.

This habitual recapitulation leads Herbert to realize that his
God's actions are in fact not arbitrary, as he had earlier pro-
posed, but that his punishments come for a reason: Herbert
has been presumptuous in growing upwards as if Heaven were
his own, and therefore he has drawn God's terrible cold wrath
upon him. We must stop to ask whether this confession of
guilt on Herbert's part is in fact a realization or an invention.
The intolerable notion of an arbitrary and occasionally malevolent God almost necessitates the invention of a human fault
to explain these punishments. That is Herbert's dilemma; either
he is guilty, and therefore deservedly punished, or he is innocent, and God is arbitrary. Faced with such a choice, he
decides for his own guilt. We cannot miss the tentative sex-
uality of his "budding" and "shooting up" and later "swelling"
—one question the poem puts is whether such self-assertion
can ever be guiltless, or whether every swelling is followed
by a punishing shriveling. The answer of the poem is equivo-

cal; his present "budding" seems innocent enough, but the inevitable alternation of spring and winter in the poem, of spring showers and icy frowns, tells us that we may always expect God's wrath. When that wrath directs itself upon the sinner,

> What frost to that? What pole is not the zone
>> Where all things burn,
>> When thou dost turn,
> And the least frown of thine is shown?

There is no more talk about keeping house snugly underground through all the hard weather. Herbert, on the contrary, has been nakedly exposed to the hard weather, has felt the freezing cold, has felt the tempests of God. The truth is out; he *has* suffered, and he still remembers his grief. Oddly, once the truth is out, Herbert has no more wish to reproach his God; he feels happier considering himself as guilty than indicting God. It is not God, he says, who is arbitrary and capricious, but we; his actions only follow ours; he is changeless, and we are the changeable ones. Herbert, having put off the old man, scarcely recognizes himself in the new man he has become:

> And now in age I bud again;
> After so many deaths I live and write;
> I once more smell the dew and rain,
> And relish versing: O my only light,
>> It cannot be
>> That I am he
> On whom thy tempests fell all night.

In the unearthly relief of this stanza, Herbert returns to the human norm. His two constant temptations are to be an angel or a plant, but the second half of "The Flower," like the second half of "Prayer," is the discovery of human truth after the self-deceptive first half. With the unforced expression of relief, Herbert can acknowledge that in truth he was not comfortably visiting underground, but was in fact being beaten by tempests. The paradisal experience of "budding again," like any paradisal experience in life, is in fact forfeit if the reality of past grief is denied: the sharpened senses that once more smell the dew and rain are those of a Lazarus newly emerged from the sepulchre; to deny the cerements is to deny the resurrection. At this point, Herbert can engage in genuine "wonder." The previous "These are thy wonders, Lord of power," may be translated "These are thy tyrannies," but now that Herbert has assuaged his anxiety by deciding that power is not arbitrary and perverse but rather solicitous and redemptive, he can say, "These are thy wonders, Lord of love." The poem is one of perfect symmetry, marked by the two poles of "wonder"; it is redundant, if one wishes to call it that, in circling back again and again to the same experience, but each time it puts that experience differently.

The end of the poem embodies yet another self-reproof on Herbert's part, put this time as a warning to all who, like himself, may have been presumptuous in thinking heaven their own:

 These are thy wonders, Lord of love,
To make us see we are but flowers that glide:
 Which, when we once can finde and prove,
Thou hast a garden for us, where to bide.
   Who would be more,
   Swelling through store,
Forfeit their Paradise by their pride.

This homiletic neatness is probably a flaw in the poem, and the very harsh judgment which Herbert passes, in this impersonal and universal way, on his earlier presumption makes this one of the comparatively rare Herbert poems with an "unhappy" ending. Since the fundamental experience of the poem is one of resurrection, and since the best lines of the poem express that sense of renewal, we may reasonably ask why these last lines are so grim. They are so, I think, because of the two truths of experience at war in the poem. One is the immediate truth of renewal and rebirth; the other is the remoter, but larger, truth of repeated self-assertion, repeated guilt, repeated punishment. Until we are "fast in Paradise," the poem tells us, we are caught in the variability of mortal life, in which, however intense renewal may be when it comes, it comes uncertainly and not for long. Intellectually, the prospect is depressing, with innocence and relish spoiled by guilt and punishment. The hell of life may continue into a hell after life. But this, since it is an intellectual conclusion, cannot fundamentally damage the wonderful sense of restored life which has made this poem famous. It speaks, however, for Herbert's grim fidelity to fact that he will not submerge the gloomy truth in the springlike experience.

The inveterate human tendency to misrepresent what has happened is nowhere more strongly criticized than in Herbert. Under his repetitive and unsparing review, all the truths finally become clear. Herbert knows that to appear pious is not to be pious; to pay formal tribute is not to love; to servilely acknowledge power is not to wonder; to utter grievances is not to pray. His readers, often mistaking the language of piety for the thing itself, are hampered by dealing with an unfamiliar discourse. We have a very rich sense of social deception in human society and can detect a note of social falseness in a novel almost before it appears; but it sometimes does not occur to us that the same equivocations, falsenesses, self-justifications, evasions, skirtings, and defensive reactions can occur in a poet's colloquies with his God. We recognize defiance when it is overt, as in "The Collar" or the first "Affliction," but other poems where the presentation is more subtle elicit bland readings and token nods to Herbert's sweetness or humility. Herbert spoke of himself as "a wonder tortur'd" and his own estimate of himself can be a guide in reading his poems.

Even in that last and most quietly worded poem, "Love," which is spoken in retrospect by the regenerate soul from the vantage point of the something understood, the old false modesty lingers. There is, as Herbert says elsewhere, no articling with God, but in this poem the soul is still refusing, in William James's words, to give up the assertion of the "little private convulsive self."[7] When Herbert catches glimpses of God's order, which we may if we wish call the best order he can imagine for himself, he finds it almost unnatural, odd— even comic. His impulse is to deny that he has any connection with such a disturbing reordering of the universe, to feel a sense of strain in attempting to accommodate himself to it, and at best, he prays that his God will remake him to fit in with that scheme, if he please: "Lord, mend or rather make us." But sometimes Herbert rejects this claim on God's indulgence. At his best, and at our best, says Herbert, God refuses to indulge the view we like to take of ourselves as hopelessly and irremediably marred and ignorant creatures. Herbert's protests that he is not capable of glory are not catered to; instead of a gentle solicitude by God, he is confronted by an equally gentle but irreducible immobility. Each of his claims to imperfection is firmly, lovingly, and even wittily put aside, and he is forced to accept God's image of him as

[7] William James, *Varieties of Religious Experience* (Boston, 1902), Ch. IV.

a guest worthy of his table. What Herbert wants is to linger
in the antechambers, to serve, to adopt any guise except the
demanding glory of the wedding garment, but Love is inflex-
ible, and the initial "humility" of the Guest is revealed as a
delusive fond clinging to his mortal dust and sin. Herbert's
God asks that he be more than what he conceives himself to
be. Herbert invented this sort of God, we may say, to embody
the demands that his own conscience put upon him, a conscience formed by that "severa parens" his mother. But even in
such a brief poem as "Love," Herbert's originality in transforming his sources, in re-inventing his topic, strikes us forcibly. We know that the poem depends on St. Luke's description of Jesus' making his disciples sit while he served them,
and on the words of the centurion transferred to the Anglican
communion service, "Lord, I am not worthy that thou
shouldst enter under my roof," and on Southwell's "S. Peter's
Complaint" (cxviii), in which St. Peter knocks on sorrow's
door and announces himself as "one, unworthy to be knowne."
We also know, from Joseph Summers, that Herbert's actual
topic is the entrance of the redeemed soul into Paradise. Now,
so far as I know, this entrance has been thought of as an
unhesitating and joyful passage, from "Come, ye blessed of
my father," to "The Saints go marching in." The link between
St. Peter knocking at a door and a soul knocking at St. Peter's door is clear, but it is Herbert's brilliance to have the
soul give St. Peter's abject response, and stand hesitant and
guilty on the threshold, just as it is a mark of his genius to
have the soul, instead of being the unworthy host at communion, be the unworthy guest in heaven. When we first read
"Love," it strikes us as exquisitely natural and humanly plaus-
ible; it is only later that the originality of conception takes
us aback. As in "Doomsday," Herbert looks at the event as it
*really* would be, not as tradition has always told us it would

be. If the redeemed soul could speak posthumously to us and tell us what its entrance into heaven was really like, what would it say? and so the process of re-invention begins.

Herbert's restless criticizing tendency coexists with an extreme readiness to begin with the cliché—roses are sweet, redeemed souls flock willingly to a heavenly banquet, sinners are swinish, Doomsday is awesome, past grief was really not too painful. On the cliché is appliquéd the critique—roses are bitter and smarting, the soul would in reality draw back from Love's table, sinners are, in desire, indistinguishable from saints, Doomsday would in fact be agreeably social, past grief was, if truth be told, intolerable. It makes very little difference to Herbert where he finds his *donnée*—in the clichés of courtly poetry, in the Bible, in his personal experience. The artless borrowed beginning becomes very soon the scrutinized personal statement. The anxiety which must have made Herbert want to begin with the safe, the bland, the familiar, and the taken-for-granted coexists permanently with the aggression which impels him almost immediately to criticize the received idea. He seems to have existed in a permanent reversible equilibrium between the two extremes of tradition and originality, diffidence and protest, the filial and the egotistic. His poems do not "resolve" these extremes into one attitude; rather they permit successive, and often mutually contradictory, expressions of the self as it explores the truth of feeling. At any moment, a poem by Herbert can repudiate itself, correct itself, rephrase itself, rethink its experience, re-invent its topic, and it is in this free play of ideas that at least part of Herbert's true originality lies.

I am grateful to the American Philosophical Society for a Grant-in-Aid which assisted the research for this essay.

W. K. WIMSATT

# Imitation as Freedom:

## 1717–1798

THE period 1717 to 1798 in England (I have chosen the dates only somewhat arbitrarily) produces poems by Pope, by Swift, by Blake, by Wordsworth and Coleridge. But many of these, and among them the most exceptional poems of the century, occur near the beginning and near the end. The critical imagination in quest of the poetical essence of this century very readily, I believe, contracts, at least momentarily, to some shorter inside period—for the sake of neatness and convenience, say, from 1744, the death of Pope, to 1784, the death of Johnson. Here in fact are found most of the characteristic lyrics of the century. This was a relatively weak or dim inner period, a poetic valley of a shadow. It is shot through, nevertheless, with many interesting flashes; it is a time full of somewhat fatigued and straining traditions, transitions, retrospective creations, hard-won, even unconscious, freedoms. One motif intrinsic to the poetry of the whole century may be observed in peculiar concentration here—the method, the bondage, and the main freedom of all English neo-classic and pre-romantic poetry—the principle of imitation or free-running parallel. Imitation not only of the full, ancient, and classical models, Homer or Pindar, Horace or Juvenal, but also, increasingly, as the classical models became, or may have seemed to become, used up, imitation of the whole British tradition and notably of the English poets who had already best imitated or paralleled the ancients—Spenser and Milton especially and, though he was still very near, Pope. Such names remind us immediately that imitation had for some decades past been enacted for the most part on a very large scale. Translated epics, georgics, or pastorals were one conspicuous, if relatively unoriginal, sort. There was more obvious originality and fun in either high or low burlesque, the various shades of mock-heroic and parody, and in the kind of free translation most often and no doubt most properly called "imitation," the satiric London parallel to Horace or Juvenal. These large-scale poems, dominantly narrative or discursive, do not of themselves tell us very much about our own specific object, the lyric. They do, however, mark out perspectives. The idea that burlesque and imitation were Augustan avenues of departure from the solemn models and constricting genre norms of the tradition, and thus of escape into a large, free realm of poetic creation, was expounded about twenty years ago by Austin Warren. I assume it as a demonstrated or at least as a persuasively argued and now more or less commonly received principle, which we can invoke to advantage—if only we keep reiterating the compensating principle that the escape from models *was* freedom, *was* expression, *was* fun, only so long as the models were preserved and were present as fields of reference for the realization of the new meanings. An imitation of a classic model is always a reference *to* and only thus a departure *from* the model. When does this mesothesis of likeness and difference succeed in being a free, original, interesting, genuine, and poetic expression? The ironies of Pope's Epistle to a blockhead Augustus give us one example of true freedom, and hence of brilliance, in the imitative mode. Some of the pieces in Dryden's collection of Juvenal translations might be adduced to illustrate the average drabness of a more literal kind of transfer.


II


The title of my paper will perhaps already have suggested the fact that I have chosen, not the method of intensive local poetic analysis, but rather that of a wider survey, with somewhat cursory allusion to select examples. June 3, 1717, is the date of Pope's first collected edition of poems—the handsome volume (in both quarto and folio) with the foldout frontispiece engraving of Pope as the straight and slender young cavalier, which along with *Eloisa to Abelard* and the "Verses to the Memory of an Unfortunate Lady" made R. K. Root say that had Pope died then, he would be remembered today as a prematurely cut-off Shelley of the Augustan age. July 13, 1717, is the date of another publication by Pope, the anonymously edited miscellany *Poems on Several Occasions*, containing a number of his own minor pieces. One of these, a poem which he was ultimately to polish into one of the few finest lyrics of the age, is a short classical imitation, the "Ode on Solitude." Later he claimed to have drafted this when he was twelve years old. "Happy the man whose wish and care/ A few paternal acres bound." The imitative virtues of this poem are not of the parodistic sort, but consist rather in its plenary, if synoptic, realization of a theme classically enshrined in Virgilian georgic, Horatian ode and epode, and Senecan chorus, in epigrams of Martial, and in Claudian's portrait of an aged farmer. The well-established medley of "retirement" images, the rural felicity and innocence, the hardihood and piety, had been rendered too by Ben Jonson, by Marvell, by Dryden, and especially by Cowley in the garland of translations with which he adorned his essays on such topics as "Obscurity," "Agriculture," and "The Dangers of an Honest Man in Much Company." Cowley's verses were favorite reading and quoting for Pope, and in the grotto and garden of his later years Pope, as we have recently been instructed in several opulent essays by Maynard Mack, was bringing off an elaborate reenactment of the ancient ideal of georgic wisdom. In what way did the stanzas of Pope, matured from his boyhood until he was nearly fifty, succeed in being free, different from, or more genuine and successful than the English translations of his predecessors? One might say, of course, that he did not translate, but made his own poem, a distillate of a whole tradition and spirit. There would be no way of refuting the assertion that almost any feature of this poem, especially any that we find subtle, novel, or pleasing, is a part of its freedom and its secret. It is with a sense of some arbitrariness, then, but perhaps not too much, that I select for comment the extraordinary freedom and éclat with which Pope has managed with the aid of meter and rhyme and phrasal parallels to tame English syntax and word order into something very much like the effects of juncture, momentary contrast, pivoting, sorting, suspension, closure, and completeness which are characteristic of Augustan Latin poetry. Such management was a tact and power of the Augustan Latin literary language. Other English poets, notably Milton throughout *Paradise Lost*, give us varied anthologies in the torment of the English language into curiously Latinate patterns. The essential refractoriness of English word order in submitting to this discipline may be illustrated in these lines from Cowley's translation of the second chorus in Seneca's *Thyestes*:

> *Me*, O ye Gods, on Earth, or else so near
> That I no Fall to Earth may fear,
> And, O ye Gods, at a good Distance *seat*
> From the long Ruins of the Great.

Pope does something different. Taking advantage of the strong points of his tiny stanza and the metrical parallels, he proceeds more smoothly, calmly, and coolly, more efficiently, in his Latinate accomplishment. A few *hints* of the Latin syntactic models are all that we need.

> *Beatus ille qui* procul negotiis,
>     ut prisca gens mortalium,
> paterna rura bobus exercet suis
>     *solutus* omni faenore
> neque excitatur classico *miles* truci . . .
>
> > Horace, *Epode* II, 1-5

> Felix, *qui* propriis aevum transegit in arvis,
> *ipsa* domus *puerum quem* vidit, *ipsa senem*.
> > Claudian, *De Sene Veronensi*, 1-2

Or, to strengthen the syntactic illustration a little, the following from a different context in Horace, but one also very well known to Pope and actually translated by him in another poem.

> vos exemplaria Graeca
> nocturna versate manu, versate diurna.
> > *Epistle to the Pisos*, 268-69

And thus:

> Happy the man whose wish and care
>   A few paternal acres bound,
> Content to breathe his native air,
>       In his own ground.
> Whose herds with milk, whose fields with bread,
>   Whose flocks supply him with attire,
> Whose trees in summer yield him shade,
>       In winter fire.

## III

The date of Pope's final revision of "Happy the Man," 1736, brings this poem within a few years of the time when Gray probably wrote a first version of his "Elegy in a Country Churchyard," and when Collins was meditating or writing his *Odes.* Gray's "Elegy" is a poem which shares very much in imagery and tone with a poem of Pope's 1717 *Works,* the "Verses [later "Elegy"] to the Memory of an Unfortunate Lady." Not only did Gray continue the Augustan line of wit, as F. R. Leavis, I believe, was the first to insist, but he was so close in time to Pope that we ought not to be surprised. The generation of Gray and Collins, the Wartons, Shenstone, Lyttelton, Akenside, Mason—in short, of the gentlemen whose poems made up Dodsley's *Collection of Poems* (1748–58)— was a generation deeply sunk in a nostalgia for the age and presence of the Augustans, and above all for Pope. Collins indeed is more patently an early romantic than Gray. Nowadays the trend is to stress his allegiance to the *Popular Super-*

*stitions,* and hence to the kind of imagination represented by fairies, witches, and hobgoblins, and to discover in his "Ode on the Poetical Character" a sort of pansexual narcissism or mythopoeic movement of identically divine and human creation. But he was recognizably a classicist too, psychologically Aeschylean and Aristotelian in his allegorical odes on the passions, and metrically both Pindaric and Horatian.

The three tetrameters and the closing dimeter of Pope's little "Ode on Solitude" were an imitation of a Horatian lyric stanza ("Ode. Sapphick," he entitled it in 1726). Collins too, in the quietest and best and best-known of his poems, the "Ode to Evening," was thinking of an ode in the Horatian sense. He chose a different, perhaps a bolder, way of approximating a Latin stanza, the Fourth Asclepiadean. Take three iambic pentameter lines, add two syllables (one foot) to the third line, and make sure that the sixth syllable (the end of the third foot) is always accented and is always the end of a word. Five, five, three, three—without rhyme. As with Horace, the stanzaic effect inheres in the varied numbers and the phrasing against the numbers. True, this kind of thing had been done in English before. It had been done first by Milton in a youthful translation, straight from Horace: "The Fifth Ode of Horace, Lib. 1. *Quis multa gracilis te puer in Rosa,* Rendered almost word for word without Rhyme according to the Latin Measure, as near as the Language will permit."

What slender Youth bedew'd with liquid odours
Courts thee on Roses in some pleasant Cave,
Pyrrha? for whom bind'st thou
In wreaths thy golden Hair . . . ?

After Milton the stanza was used not only by Collins but somewhat stiffly by all three of the Wartons, who wore it, as

Oliver Elton says, almost like the badge of a group. "Only
Collins," he says, "brought out its music." The greater freedom, the finer tone, of Collins's stanzas to the "nymph re-
served," "chaste Eve" ("Now teach me, maid compos'd,/ To
breathe some soften'd strain") come in part through his novel
extension of a classic form to enclose or shape the stuff of a
newly intensified landscape melancholy—a mood, as Yvor
Winters argues, that subsists purely in its symbols, with no
real motives. (Perhaps not so new at that, but a subtly modu-
lated old, Miltonic stuff.) This poem is a deepened version of
the retirement theme. One free formal feature to be noted
about it is surely that, whereas the dim landscape images and
pensive mood are minor Miltonic, the movement of the phrases
through the tiny stanzas is not cut or segmented, as in "Pen-
seroso" couplets, but is like the actual movement of Horatian
odes and at the same time like Milton's *Paradise Lost* style
and his sonnet style too, continuous from line to line, and
even from stanza to stanza.

> ... some soften'd Strain,
> Whose Numbers stealing thro' thy darkning Vale,
> May not unseemly with its Stillness suit,
> As musing slow, I hail
> Thy genial lov'd Return!

We can see an instructive sort of contrast to Collins's well-
known verses in another "Ode to Evening," included in the
twin small volume of odes published simultaneously in Decem-
ber, 1746, by his Winchester and Oxford friend, Joseph Warton.

> Hail, meek-eyed maiden, clad in sober gray,
> Whose soft approach the weary woodman loves

As, homeward bent to kiss his prattling babes,
He jocund whistles through the twilight groves.

Content with forgoing the rhyme of the first and third lines,
this pentameter quatrain insists, nevertheless, on a square
enough parallel, balanced halving of lines, and stanzaic closure
to illustrate a minor poetic strain that was tuning quietly during the decade toward its sudden and plenary fulfillment in
Gray's "Elegy." The "Colin Clout" or "Nosce Teipsum" quatrain of alternating rhymes had been employed by D'Avenant
and Dryden at the middle of the preceding century as a counterpart of classical heroic hexameters, somewhat ampler than
the English couplet. It was a relatively obscure and very weak
poet, James Hammond, who about 1732, in a sequence of
expurgated Tibullan adaptations, seems first to have conceived
this quatrain as a counterpart of the Latin hexameter and pentameter, or elegiac couplet—fit metrical emblem for the pensive melancholy of frustrate love. William Shenstone, who
alluded to the stanza as "Hammond's meter," wrote more of
the same sort of watery elegies, twenty-six in number, and an
introductory theoretical essay upon the genre. How did Gray
succeed at one leap in carrying this slender tradition so far
beyond the "necessities" or timidities which had hitherto
seemed to constrain it? Geoffrey Tillotson suggests that one
of Gray's inventions is the landscape picture laid down in separate strips, line by line.

The lowing herd winds slowly o'er the lea,
The plowman homeward plods his weary way.

True, we have noted the same thing in Warton's relatively
tame "Ode to Evening." Still, it may be that these landscape
strips, as Gray manages them, are a notable part of his unique

quality. Gray's "Elegy" shares with Pope's a preservative technique in blending the softness of elegiac feeling with the tartness of satiric commentary. Cleanth Brooks has observed the ironic reciprocation between country churchyard and the funerary emblems of the great abbey church. Perhaps we shall be tempted to say that Gray transcends and outdoes Hammond and Shenstone simply because he writes a more poetic line, richer, fuller, more resonant and memorable in all the ways in which we are accustomed to analyze the poetic quality. There may be no other way of describing his poetic freedom. I would not debate long against that. Let me, however, add one more observation (I note it too in Brooks's essay and in a more recent essay by Bertrand Bronson), that the resonance and fullness of this poem in the memory come in good part from the concluding personal complement to, and affirmation of, the marmoreally impersonal main statement. The universalized meditation comes home, as Johnson said, to the reader's business and bosom through the final focus and intensification in the heart of the speaker himself, who sees (and, as Brooks argues, *chooses*) his own grave and epitaph. ("For thee, who mindful of th' unhonour'd Dead/ Dost in these lines their artless tale relate . . ." not Gray in any special personal sense, of course, not West, and not a village stonecutter—but the melancholy, sensitive unknown poet meditator and speaker—and hence you, I, we, anybody who happens to be reading the poem.) One reason why I come to rest on this idea is that it affords, I believe, a very instructive moment of comparison with one of Gray's two Pindaric odes, "The Progress of Poesy."

The Pindaric ode in English was one of the straightest or most serious ways of imitating the classic model. The sublimity of the models almost precluded the kind of freedom and significant parodic fun that was invited by satire and epic. Or if parody was attempted, as by Bonnell Thornton in his burlesque St. Cecilia's Day ode set to music by Dr. Arne for Ranelagh in 1763, and by Lloyd and Colman in *Two Odes* (1760) ridiculing Gray and Mason, it almost necessarily fell to an extreme of contrast; it was low travesty. Dryden, improving on the neo-classic "free verse" of Cowley, had demonstrated a kind of bravura of musical mimesis, a wildly recitative ring, in two irregular St. Cecilia's Day odes. Pope, despite his admiration for Dryden's feat in the *Essay on Criticism*, had done less than his best in an attempt at the same genre, published in 1713. Edward Young contrived weak adaptations of Dryden's style, in sublime celebration of the British navy (1728–34).[1] Congreve had earlier (1706) come in to assert briefly that the Pindaric ode ought in fact to be a very regular three-phase construct—strophe, antistrophe, and epode (turn, counterturn, and stand, as Ben Jonson had put it), precisely repeated in successive triads. The lesson had been not much noticed for another thirty years. But with the *Odes* of Collins and Warton and the even more recent translation of Pindar by Gilbert West (1749), Gray was in a position to go all out in a highly intricate (countable and testable though probably never really audible) triadic pattern, precisely repeated, and to add to this formidably classic quality a range and depth of allusiveness which in the collected *Poems* of 1768 he permitted himself to cover with a panoply of footnotes such as American students of the present age are likely to associate with the *Waste Land* of Eliot. There *was* a kind of

[1] The episode is described by E. E. Reimer in his unpublished Yale doctoral dissertation of 1968, "The Paradoxical Sublime: Edward Young's Early Works," Ch. V.

freedom in all this, a bold originality—to which we find the
most thunderous testimony in the outrage vented by Samuel
Johnson: ". . . glittering accumulations of ungraceful orna-
ments; they strike, rather than please; . . . the language is
laboured into harshness. . . . 'Double, double, toil and trouble.'
He has a kind of strutting dignity, and is tall by walking on
tiptoe."

But to return to the connection with the "Elegy" which I
began by hinting: the boldest, by far the most striking and
shocking thing about "The Progress of Poesy" seems to me
to be the closing stanza, the epode of the third triad, bringing to a conclusion, or up to the latest date, the progress of
poesy from Greece through Italy to England, Shakespeare,
Milton, Dryden. Thus far have the "paths of glory" led. At
the end of the "Elegy," the humble poet-speaker, the melancholy "youth to fortune and to fame unknown," was lying
flat, in his grave, his "head upon the lap of earth," his "frail-
ties" sunk in "the bosom of his Father and his God." (So far
as obscurity is a choice, it is a choice which Nature cooper-
ates all too readily in helping us to make.) But the "youth
pined away with desire," as a later vision will instruct us,
does "arise from [his] grave and aspire,/ Where [the] sun-
flower wishes to go." The end of "The Progress of Poesy" is
another ending of one poet's recital, but the end of a far big-
ger story also. No "mute inglorious" Miltons have appeared
in the cast of characters, but "he" himself "that rode sublime/
Upon the seraph-wings of Extasy." And now, today, in 1754?

> Oh! Lyre divine, what daring Spirit
> Wakes thee now? Tho' he inherit
> Nor the pride, nor ample pinion,
> That the Theban Eagle bear . . .

Yet oft before his infant eyes would run
Such forms, as glitter in the Muse's ray
With orient hues, unborrow'd of the Sun:
Yet shall he mount, and keep his distant way
Beyond the limits of a vulgar fate,
Beneath the Good how far—but far above the Great.

The epitaph which concludes the churchyard "Elegy," I have argued, transcends or envelops the merely individual. It is the individual focus of the universal. Can the same be said for the galvanic resurrection which concludes the daring third epode of "The Progress of Poesy"? I think not. For, after all, it is our common fate to be dead and to lie flat in the ground. It is a very special and eminent experience to mount and soar, even though a little lower than the Theban eagle, yet "beyond the limits of a vulgar fate." Gray, one might plead, is not thinking of himself, but just of the sublime English poet of the moment, whoever he may be. But who else could he be at this moment, as this triumphant epode is penned? The stanza to my mind is rampant with the individuality, and the vanity, of the Cambridge scholar! In this it displays a very unusual degree of correctly wild Pindaric energy. Nevertheless, it may seem, and be, like the rest of the ode, cold enough for us, even repellent. Freedom, we may wonder, but as in many a political issue, freedom to do what?

Gray's second Pindaric ode, "The Bard," equally intricate and regular, is another celebration of the power and progress of poesy, urged with an even more intense degree of rhapsodic energy. The frenzied Welsh bard, joined in dreadful harmony by a chorus of ghostly colleagues, pronounces a doom upon the royal line of Edward I but adds a prophecy of long poetic glories for England under the Tudors. "Robed

in a sable garb of woe,/ With haggard eyes the Poet stood;/
Loose his beard, and hoary hair . . ." Every schoolboy knows,
or once knew, that he punctuates his tirade by a leap from
the side of Snowdon into the Conway's foaming flood. The
visionary bardic afflatus, a form of wit to madness near allied,
was appropriate matter for the throb of the wild Pindaric
strophe. If one way to freedom was the irresponsibility of
parody and burlesque, another way, known or hinted at since
classic times, was madness. It was good, at any rate, as a literary device.[2] Perhaps it was even better in actuality. The
date of Horace Walpole's inaugural of the printing press at
Strawberry Hill with Gray's two odes, 1757, was also the
approximate date when another Cambridge scholar, a prolific
London hack writer, went really mad, or at any rate entered
a period of confinement in several madhouses. Christopher
Smart's antiphonal logbook, *Jubilate Agno* (*Rejoice in the
Lamb*), written during this time, recovered and published long
after, bears the marks of a genuinely mad mind. It bears also
the unmistakable marks of poetic genius.

> For I will consider my Cat Jeoffry.
> For he is a servant of the Living God duly and daily serving
>     him.
> For at the first glance of the glory of God in the East he
>     worships in his way.
>
>        .     .     .
>
> For when his day's work is done his business more properly
>     begins.
> For he keeps the Lord's watch in the night against the
>     adversary.

[2] Cf. Raymond D. Havens, "Assumed Personality, Insanity, and
Poetry," *RES*, New Series, IV (January, 1953), 26–36.

For he counteracts the powers of darkness by his electrical
   skin & glaring eyes.
For he has the subtlety and hissing of a serpent, which in
   goodness he suppresses.
For he will not do destruction, if he is well-fed, neither will
   he spit without provocation.
For he purrs in thankfulness, when God tells him he's a
   good Cat.

To my mind there is more poetic life in these disjunct anti-
phons than in either of Gray's intricately labored odes. What
makes the poetic freedom and success of this passage? To
speak roughly: loving and amused observation of a household
animal is coupled with the sacramental view of the universe
and the prayerful form of Scripture and liturgy. The freedom
arises in a reverently irreverent parody of Scripture and the
Prayer Book. Madness was the interior dynamic that issued
the license for this kind of parody.

IV

With Gray's Pindaric odes and Samuel Johnson's imitation
of the Tenth Satire of Juvenal a few years earlier, we arrive
at an approximate climax and end to the direct and straight
imitation of the classics in the English neo-classical movement.
To carry our narration of freedom through imitation any
further, we need now a new rubric, a new term or two—
none the less valid because they may be our own favorite
terms, rather than those the age would most readily have ap-

plied to itself. I am thinking of some such terms as *antiquar-
ianism*[3] and *primitivism*.

Percy's *Reliques of Ancient English Poetry* (1765) will immediately come to mind, and in connection with this it is
worth our while to notice in passing one kind of native or
folk freedom which flourished in that enlightened age but
which an age of modern scholars seems hardly to have sus-
pected until Bertrand Bronson brought it to light about twen-
ty-three years ago in his account of Mrs. Brown of Falkland,
who was a ballad informant of Sir Walter Scott's informants
William Tytler and Alexander Fraser Tytler, Lord Wood-
houselee. Daughter of a professor at Aberdeen and wife of a
clergyman, this lady carried in her head, from singing heard
in childhood, no fixed or bookish text of a ballad, but just the
ballad itself, a narrative line or story poem (a "fluid entity")
which she felt free to cast and recast in numerous rhetorical
and prosodic variations.[4] In this instance, the freedom seems
to have produced no important creative results. But it may
help us to appreciate the fact that we are indebted to free
sources of the same kind for those sharply trimmed essential
versions of "Edward" and "Sir Patrick Spens" which an earlier Scottish collector, Boswell's friend Lord Hailes, had given
to Percy. There is no reason to think these were any more
ancient or more genuine than any of the numerous inferior
versions of the same ballads which may be found in Child and
Sharp. They were the work of living eighteenth-century Scottish reciters. The vital energy of the age in traditional song, as
Bronson says, put forth natural "flowers—proper to the season,

[3] "A mere Antiquarian is a rugged being" (Samuel Johnson in
Boswell's *Life*, 1778).
[4] "Mrs. Brown and the Ballad," *California Folklore Quarterly*, IV
(April, 1945), 129–40.

not excavated fossils." The eighteenth century no less than the fifteenth was "a golden age" of Scottish balladry.

But in naming Percy I have in mind mainly another kind of freedom—one very effective way in which even the bookish poet could escape the rigors of the prevailing civilized norms of elegance and good sense. This was somewhat like the way of imitation and burlesque. I mean the escape which Percy enjoyed by the simple, half-apologetic act of electing to put before the public the rude rhymes of an earlier uncouth age. He and his readers could thus innocently disport themselves in all this raciness and vigor. The harshness and uncouthness were not their responsibility. True, some of the pieces had to be touched up a little by Percy and made more presentable. But this too was a form of connivance and participation, of fiction, and hence of freedom.

Percy's first edition of the *Reliques,* let us recall, was closely contemporary with the Gaelic pseudo-documents of another Scottish antiquary, James Macpherson, and the rhythmic English prose translations which he produced in three volumes as the poems of the ancient Fenian poet Ossian.[5] "We gave the song to the kings. A hundred harps mixed their sound with our voice." The plushy green headlands, the blue bays, the wind groaning in the pines and oaks, the ships, halls, caves, tombs, and campfires, the running deer and boars, the thrusting and the bleeding warriors, the spears, swords, harps, armor, and gems—the whole bardic idiom of Homeric and Miltonic imitation—constituted a distinct poetic invention on the part of Macpherson, if no very subtle one. He gained the freedom to indulge in this invention through the removal and protection of his fictive plunge of fifteen centuries.

[5] The date of the sixteen *Fragments* is 1760, that of the epic poem *Fingal,* in six books, 1762, that of *Temora,* in eight books, 1763.

A very similar element of freedom in forgery appears in the more sympathetic fraud committed not much later by Thomas Chatterton, the sad and marvelous Bristol boy. The three posthumous editions of his *Rowley Poems*, by the eminent Chaucerian Thomas Tyrwhitt, the third containing the solid philological exposure, appeared in 1777 and 1778. Chatterton's Rowley poems were an orphan's pathological flight from present reality into an archaic world of fine fabling and of plangent filial yearning.

> Sprytes of the bleste, on goulden trones astedde
> Poure oute yer pleasaunce own mie fadres hedde.

More important for the formal side of our inquiry, Chatterton used the sanction of a mock antique vocabulary and grammar to create a new kind of free poetic idiom. Like the Spenser of Ben Jonson's phrase, Chatterton-Rowley "writ no language." And yet, like Spenser, he did write a language, and marvelously well. He wrote his own expressionistic fusion of contemporary English and certain freely mingled echoes of the past. The elements, the phonemes and the morphemes, as we might say today, were all pure English. The way they were run together was the oddity and the achievement, something legitimized by the supposed antiquity, but in large part determined by a rhythmic and expressive tact which, if it has to be explained in brief, we may attempt to explain by an appeal to a principle expounded, in humorous fantasy a hundred years later, as "Jabberwocky." The effects are only in part orthographic and ocular.

> Whanne Englonde, smeethynge from her lethal wounde,
> From her gall'd necke dyd twytte the chayne awaie,

Kennynge her legeful sonnes fall all arounde,
(Myghtie theie fell, 'Twas Honoure ledde the fraie,)
Thanne inne a dale, bie eve's dark surcote graie,
Twayne lonelie shepsterres dyd abrodden flie,
(The rostlyng liff doth theyr whytte hartes affraie,)
And wythe the owlette trembled and dyd crie . . .

Eclogue I, Stanza I

The featherd songster chaunticleer
    Han wounde hys bugle horne,
And told the earlie villager
    The commynge of the morne.

"Bristowe Tragedie: Or the Dethe<br>of Syr Charles Bawdin," Stanza I.

A great nineteenth-century scholar, the Reverend W. W. Skeat, tried to get at the essence of Chatterton's Rowley poems —"the exact amount of merit" to which Chatterton had "attained"—by translating them into correct modern English. "Han" is a plural verb in Chaucerian English, not singular. And thus we get:

The feathered songster chanticleer
    Has wound his bugle horn.

And thus in the interest of grammar is obliterated whatever charm the tiny alliterative clarion of the line may have had.

It may seem too big a leap (in poetic idiom even if not in chronology) from Chatterton to the publication in 1786 at Kilmarnock in Ayrshire of Robert Burns's *Poems, Chiefly in the Scottish Dialect*. But I believe there are good reasons for mentioning Burns immediately after Chatterton. Whatever we may wish to say about the racy and earthy peasant freedom of

Burns's poems and his free lyric lilt and gusto, the language in
which he wrote (when he was not writing like James Thomson, in the Spenserian stanzas of "The Cotter's Saturday
Night"), the Lowland Scots dialect, whatever precisely that is,
is of great importance for understanding the free expressive
power which Burns enjoyed. The eighteenth century, we
know, was full of humble and uneducated poets—in Pope's
time Stephen Duck, the Poetical Thresher; later Henry Jones,
the Poetical Bricklayer; Mrs. Ann Yearsley, of Bristol, the
Poetical Milk-Woman, Lactilla; James Woodhouse, the Poetical Shoemaker. And others too. The marvelous thing about all
these poets was that, although of lowly origin and meager op-
portunity, they wrote the standard style of high varnish and
poetic diction, like all the other bad and mediocre poets of the
era. That was their achievement. The marvelous thing about
Burns, on the contrary, was that, being a peasant, he managed
to write in what was apparently the language of a peasant. But
just how precisely or literally he wrote in such a language, or,
so far as he did, what were its peculiar capacities for poetic
expression, is a difficult question. Is such a language an initial
opaque obstacle to understanding, which the English reader, by
historical linguistic research, penetrates, in order to get at a
hidden rich meaning? Or is it not possible that in some way
such a language is in fact a specially and immediately expressive medium, a contrivance for a much more direct, if inex-
plicit, presentation, than the civilized literary language permits?
Let me suggest the nature of this problem by quoting first a
few lines from an early Scottish contemporary of Burns,
Robert Fergusson, who died young in 1774, a university and
city man and a satirical poet of the city, Edinburgh. Still he
wrote also of the country, as in the following lines from his
poem entitled "The Farmer's Ingle."

Niest the gude wife her hireling damsels bids
    Glowr thro' the byre, and see the hawkies bound,
Take tent case Crummy tak her wonted tids,
    And ca' the leglen's treasure on the ground,
    Whilk spills a kebbuck nice, or yellow pound.

A student, even a serious college student, would have trouble understanding those lines, written in a very genuine, unquestionable eighteenth-century Scots. *Hawkies, Crummy, tids, leglen, kebbuck?* The passage is about a farm wife, her milkmaids, and her cows. And now, by contrast, a few lines from Burns. From "Tam o' Shanter" (1791):

O Tam had'st thou but been sae wise,
As taen thy ain wife Kate's advice!
She tauld thee well thou wast a skellum
A blethering, blustering, drunken blellum.

From a poetical epistle to a friend, in the 1786 volume:

O, sweet are Coila's haughs an' woods,
When lintwhites chant amang the buds,
And jinkin hares, in amorous whids,
    Their loves enjoy;
While thro' the braes the cushat croods
    With wailfu' cry!

Here again the words may be strange to us, but I dare say they will scarcely seem an obstacle to our getting a strong impression of what the passages are saying. The country Scots chosen by Burns and mixed with literary Scots and with straight English is for the most part not an opaque language to us, nor was it to Wordsworth or Keats, who in 1803 and 1818 wrote

poems at Burns's grave. Nor do I think it could have been to
Burns's English contemporaries, nor to the Edinburgh literati
(despite a gesture of glossing in Mackenzie's review). The
glossary prefixed to the Kilmarnock volume by Burns himself
may be taken as a part of the act. Burns's dialect in his best-
known poems—his vocabulary of the wee, the sleekit, timorous,
cowrin, and generally comic and sympathetic diminutive, or at
an opposite pole, of the braw, fou, blethering, blustering,
blellum and skellum—is very largely transparent to an educated
English reader. (Some of the pleasure which we get from it is
very similar to that which we get on recognizing slapstick and
indecent jokes in Shakespeare.) Let us remember again the
principle of Jabberwocky. "How high browse thou, brown
cow?"[6]

## V

Imitation or burlesque of the Greek and Roman classic
models. Imitation or forgery of the British archaic past or the
primitive present. A third strain of imitation, as we noticed at
the start, was imitation of the English classics, from Chaucer to
Pope, or in a broader sense, imitation of the classic tradition.
Sometimes free and expressive, sometimes a mere nostalgic
exercise! At this point, if we had space for a longer narrative,
William Shenstone's picturesque and humorous Spenserian
*Schoolmistress* (in three versions, 1737 and after) might be
praised at the expense of William Mason's more simply nos-

[6] The matters on which I touch briefly here are in the course of
being treated at length by Mr. James McArdle in a dissertation on
the poetic language of Burns.

talgic Chaucerian, Spenserian, and Miltonic parodies in his *Monody on the Death of Pope.* An unobtrusive pastoral strain, imitative and classical, might be traced from Pope and Gay through Collins, Churchill, Goldsmith, and Chatterton, to Crabbe's anti-pastoral *Village* of 1783. And we might dwell for a little upon the curiously half-conscious debt of William Cowper to Pope in his satiric *Table Talk* (1782) and (after John Philips and Thomson) his debt to Milton in his georgic *Task* (1785). Such a detour away from the lyric, if we could afford it, would deepen, but is perhaps not needed to define, the context of imitative and parodistic assumptions which enveloped the production of the next volume of lyrics that I want to notice. It is a fact I believe not often dwelt on that George Crabbe's sourly antitraditional yet conservatively fashioned poem *The Village* appeared in the same year, 1783, as the small volume of juvenile poems, *Poetical Sketches,* printed and distributed to a few friends by the young London engraver William Blake. These were written, according to the Advertisement, between his twelfth and his twentieth year. The earliest of them, that is, may have been written about 1769, the year before the death of Chatterton. The latest must have been written a little later than Blake's twentieth year, for there would seem to be debts to Chatterton's *Rowley Poems* (1777), and to his *Miscellanies* (1778).[7] These poems, we remember, are miscellaneous, odd, rough-seeming, ragged, bold ("full of irregularities and defects," says the Advertisement)— a wider range of imitative experiments than anything we have so far consulted. They include rhythmic prose in the manner of Ossian (or of Chatterton's imitations of Ossian) and of the King James Bible; a nightmare pseudo-Gothic ballad, a mad

[7] F. W. Bateson, *Selected Poems of William Blake* (New York, 1957), pp. 93–100.

song, and a song of frustrated love, all these in the manner
more or less of Percy's *Reliques;* a large fragment of a Shakespearean history play, *Edward III;* a Miltonic prologue; a
mythological poem in a sequence of variously approximate
Spenserian stanzas; and, perhaps most impressive of all, opening
the volume, a set of apostrophes to the four seasons, blended in
a new and strangely lyric way from James Thomson, Milton,
the Song of Solomon, and no doubt other sources. It is difficult
to imagine what Dr. Johnson would have said of this volume
of subcultural expressions if a copy had chanced to come into
his hands. Blake took his liberties, right and left. One of the
most obvious formal, if superficial, examples is that of the successive deviations in the Spenserian stanzas.[8] Here I should say
the expressive effect is nearly zero. But it is not difficult to find,
though it may require some tact to analyze, examples near the
opposite end of the value scale. About twenty years ago
Cleanth Brooks published in the *CEA Critic*[9] an essay showing
how the song of frustrated love, "My silks and fine array," is a
job of sweet-sad ritual cunning performed in variations upon
Elizabethan lyrics of the Walsingham type which Blake's copy
of Percy's *Reliques* at Wellesley College suggests that he knew
very well. At about the same time, I myself made the observation, which has been, I believe, well enough received by the
guardians of the field, that one deeply and freely romantic
feature of the apostrophe "To Spring" is the remarkable fusion
yet division of the imagery whereby the biblical lover descends
into and is blended with a native landscape, which also bears

---

[8] The imitative manner of *Poetical Sketches* was first extensively
studied, with a strong accent on detection of sources, by Margaret
Ruth Lowery in her Yale doctoral dissertation, directed by C. B.
Tinker, *Windows of the Morning* (New Haven, 1940).

[9] XII, No. 9 (October, 1950), 1–6.

the image of his waiting bride. In a curious variant of the method, the fiery Apollonian tyrant King Summer descends upon the land, only to be invited to seek relief in a nap under an oak or a swim in a river.

The happy manner in which such mythic fusions join Miltonic meter and syntax to make the freedom and originality of Blake the youthful experimenter can, as it happens, be suggested *ab extra* by contrast with a little-known poem which Blake's "To Spring" seems in part to have inspired. William Stanley Roscoe was the son of a Liverpool banker who in his spare moments was an editor of Pope, a patron of the arts, and a friend of friends of William Blake. The younger Roscoe's poem "To Spring, on the Banks of the Cam," written presumably in his youth, about 1800, though published only in his *Poems* of 1834, combines the stanza of Collins's "Ode to Evening" with Blake's abruptly orotund apostrophic opening.

> O thou that from the green vales of the West
> Comst in thy tender robes with bashful feet,
> And to the gathering clouds
> Liftest thy soft blue eye:
> I woo thee, Spring!

I do not undertake to prove or even adequately to illustrate the thesis that Roscoe's poem is not a very good one. But it is not. It can be consulted in Brooks and Warren's *Understanding Poetry*, or in the *Oxford Book of Victorian Verse*. It deserves, I believe, special notice as perhaps the only instance of direct, exemplary influence which can be claimed for Blake's half-suppressed *Sketches*.[10]

[10] Arnold Goldman, "Blake and the Roscoes," *Notes and Queries,* CCX (May, 1965), 178–82.

More recently, Harold Bloom, in probably the most sustained critical gaze yet directed upon Blake's *Sketches*, has observed the "small . . . humanizing" scale of the two Spenserian epithalamic apostrophes "To the Evening Star" and "To Morning"; the "sexual paradise and trap" of the garden in the Song: "How sweet I roam'd"; conventional poetic diction turned on itself in the "gently mocking" "To the Muses"; Shakespearean winter pastoral joined with the genial manner of Goldsmith in "Blind Man's Buff."

Blake's *Poetical Sketches* is a volume saturated with the English poetic tradition from the Elizabethan age through the mid-eighteenth century, brimming with imitative exuberance, and thus wildly and torrentially free. We might almost be tempted to think in a careless moment that it is only accidentally, crudely, and boyishly free. It would be difficult to think of a single small volume more happily illustrative of the half-genetic, half-critical argument I have been trying to push: that the expressive freedom of eighteenth-century English poetry is born only in virtue of the mimetic and repetitive tradition under which the poets labored. This volume is surely, as Harold Bloom would say, "premonitory" of the two strikingly original yet imitative lyric collections which would follow before the end of the century. Blake's *Songs of Innocence and of Experience* is perhaps most readily located by a new reader in its superficially traditional and formal aspects, the meters and the language of childish songs, the "hymns unbidden." Its radical and explosive originality lies at difficult depths. The emblematic character of the form, as John Hollander says, is used to cover a shift in the character of the content. The poems of Coleridge and Wordsworth in *Lyrical Ballads*, and especially those of Wordsworth, seemed from the start, or were said from the start, and mainly by Wordsworth himself, to be a conspicuous departure from all that was expected of poems by a reader tamed in the eighteenth-century popular tradition. "Every author, as far as he is great and at the same time *original*," Wordsworth would later say, "has had the task of *creating* the taste by which he is to be enjoyed."[11] But Coleridge would qualify that. In the *Biographia* he argued that a clamor of protest over *Lyrical Ballads* had been aroused more by Wordsworth's extreme theoretical statements than by the poems themselves. Within recent years an American scholar, Robert Mayo, has demonstrated, I think, that in all the superficials of both form and content, *Lyrical Ballads* was representative of what had already grown to be a "persistent" minority segment of the magazine verse of the 1790s. Bereaved, deserted, and vagrant females, mendicants of both sexes, old soldiers, convicts, unfortunate rustics of every sort, are frequent protagonists in those pages. Insanity and simplicity, picturesque scenery, topographical meditation, humanitarianism, and sentimental morality are dominant motifs in poems which assume the forms of ballad, "lyric," complaint, fragment, sketch, anecdote, expostulation and reply, occasional inscription.[12]

Old Sarah lov'd her helpless child,
   Whom helplessness made dear,
And life was happiness to him,
   Who had no hope or fear.

[11] *Essay Supplementary to the Preface*, 1815, seventh paragraph from the end. The letter to Lady Beaumont of May 21, 1807, last paragraph, attributes the same idea to Coleridge, in nearly the same words.

[12] Robert Mayo, "The Contemporaneity of the *Lyrical Ballads*," *PMLA*, LXIX (June, 1954), 480–522.

She knew his wants, she understood
    Each half artic'late call,
And he was everything to her,
    And she to him was all.

Not a rejected Wordsworthian fragment from *Lyrical Ballads*
—but part of a poem entitled "The Idiot" in the *Sporting
Magazine* for October, 1798.[13] When compared with earlier
eighteenth-century primitives, Stephen Duck, Henry Jones,
Ann Yearsley, or even Robert Burns, Wordsworth may seem
to achieve his originality, as he claims, by the simple expedient
of using a selection of the language of ordinary men—a plain,
prosy middle sort of standard English—albeit informed by
some special excitement. When he is compared with some of
his more immediate contemporaries, however, this kind of
originality largely disappears. Wordsworth's freedom and originality, whether in a poem of poetic diction, such as "Tintern
Abbey," or in his plainest ballad narrations, will be found ultimately to consist in the fact that he is a better poet than most
of his contemporaries at most moments. He has "the original
gift of spreading the tone." He writes with more force and
interest, even with more "wit," if I dare use such a term. This
is the essence of poetic freedom.

[13] *Ibid.*, p. 499.

ॐॐ A. REEVE PARKER

# Wordsworth's Whelming Tide:

## COLERIDGE AND THE ART OF ANALOGY

ॐॐ OF Coleridge's later meditative poems, the most notable is "To William Wordsworth," written at Coleorton in January, 1807, after Wordsworth had recited his poem "on the growth of an individual Mind." Traditionally, readers have found it a window on Coleridge's personality, and have heard in its "confession voice" an uneven but moving *cri de coeur*.[1]

Ah! as I listened with a heart forlorn,
The pulses of my being beat anew:
And even as Life returns upon the drowned,
Life's joy rekindling roused a throng of pains—
Keen pangs of Love, awakening as a babe
Turbulent, with an outcry in the heart;
And fears self-willed, that shunned the eye of Hope;

[1] Cf. Max F. Schulz, *The Poetic Voices of Coleridge* (Detroit, 1963), pp. 132–34. Quotations from "To William Wordsworth" are from *Poetical Works*, ed. E. H. Coleridge (Oxford, 1912). Numbers in parentheses identify the first line of each passage.

And Hope that scarce would know itself from Fear;
Sense of past Youth, and Manhood come in vain,
And Genius given, and Knowledge won in vain;
And all which I had culled in wood-walks wild,
And all which patient toil had reared, and all,
Commune with thee had opened out—but flowers
Strewed on my corse, and borne upon my bier,
In the same coffin, for the self-same grave!                    (61)

Hearing Wordsworth read what Dorothy called "the poem
to Coleridge" might well have overwhelmed the artist in him.
*The Prelude* was, after all, the masterly product of years when
Coleridge's own poetic creativity was most painfully in abey-
ance, his mind most subject to despair. The Malta experiment
had failed. He arrived at Coleorton in precarious health, still
using opium, and without money or prospects. The continuing
distress of working out a separation from his wife and children
was intensified by the apparent harmony of the Wordsworth
household, for him the embodiment of everything he so desper-
ately idealized in human relations. For years, from 1797 when
Coleridge heard "The Ruined Cottage" at Racedown to the
evenings in 1807 when he again listened, this time to a poem he
had helped conceive, the intimacy of William's world, which
now included Wordsworth's sister-in-law, Sara Hutchinson,
charmed and excluded him. The stimulating friendship with
Wordsworth himself cost Coleridge dearly. He invested
Wordsworth with a power destructive of his own self-assurance. The older poet became little less than a father-figure,
focus of the ambivalent affection and rivalry such oedipal
transferences produce. Shortly after his arrival at Coleorton,
for example, Coleridge's neurotic fantasy coupled William and
Sara in an unthinkable adultery that for Coleridge had all the
taboo of incest.

Such psycho-biographical considerations pertain to an adequate reading of "To William Wordsworth." But they do not comprehend the nature of the poem, which is more than a transparent expression of distress. Beyond question, the "personality" is there: in 1815 Coleridge himself reassured Wordsworth, who feared embarrassment if the poem was published, that he

> wanted no additional reason for its not being published in my Life Time, than it's *personality* respecting myself—After the opinions, I had given publicly, for the preference of the Lycidas (moral no less than poetical) to Cowley's Monody, I could not have printed it consistently—. It is for the Biographer, not the Poet, to give the *accidents* of *individual* Life. What ever is not representative, generic, may indeed be poetically exprest, but is not Poetry.[2]

The aesthetic argument may have been a pretext to allay Wordsworth's fears, for if Coleridge had not already done so, in a few months he decided to publish the poem in *Sibylline Leaves*, with Wordsworth's identity only thinly veiled.[3] But he also did what he could to rid the poem of purely personal and accidental elements, since for him the poem was never merely an egregiously autobiographical lament. However, readers have neglected its "representative" and "generic" nature. And the illustration of "Lycidas" was no casual gesture in his letter, as Wordsworth knew. There is an important artistic design in "To William Wordsworth," but it cannot be discerned by criticism focusing primarily on tone and diction and operating

[2] *Collected Letters*, ed. E. L. Griggs (Oxford, 1956–    ), IV, 572.
[3] He had already written to Joseph Cottle and Lord Byron about the collection that became *Sibylline Leaves*. See *Collected Letters*, IV, 546–47, 551–52, 559–63.

on the premise that structure and style in romantic poetry are chiefly expressions of psychological forces in the poet's personality.

This is not to say that Coleridge's inclination as a poet (or critic) was toward objectivist formalism. He was the most purposefully egotistic writer of his day, and the aim of this essay is to explore the subtle egotism of his poem to Wordsworth. As early as 1796 he defended egotism in his poems: "If I could judge of others by myself, I should not hesitate to affirm, that the most interesting passages in our most interesting poems are those in which the Author develops his own feelings." But there was a difference between "personality," dealing with the "*accidents* of *individual* Life," and its development into egotism. True egotism was not idiosyncratic or accidental. On such grounds in 1819 he acknowledged the weakness of another poem, the "Hymn Before Sunrise," as consisting

> in the Author's addressing himself to *individual* objects actually present to his Senses while his great predecessors apostrophize *classes* of Things, presented by the memory and generalized by the understanding.[4]

At the end of his life, he was still elaborating the same insight:

> In the Paradise Lost—indeed, in every one of his poems—it is Milton himself whom you see; his Satan, his Adam, his Raphael, almost his Eve—all are John Milton; and it is a sense of this intense egotism that gives me the greatest pleasure in reading Milton's works. The egotism of such a man is a revelation of spirit.[5]

[4] *Collected Letters*, IV, 974.
[5] *Table Talk*, August 18, 1833, in *Collected Works*, ed. W. G. T. Shedd (New York, 1854), VI, 479.

Like Wordsworth, Milton was a figure of awesome authority whose genius inspired Coleridge. (He often compared them.) "What joy to meet a Milton in a future state, &, with that reverence due to a superior, pour forth our deep thanks for the noble feelings, he had aroused in us." But such reverence was also problematic for an imagination bent on competing and able to discern in the mirror of Milton's career an accusing reflection of his own plight:

> No one can rise from the perusal of this immortal poem [*Paradise Lost*] without a deep sense of the grandeur and the purity of Milton's soul, or without feeling how suscepti- ble of domestic enjoyments he really was, notwithstanding the discomforts which actually resulted from an apparently unhappy choice in marriage. He was, as every truly great poet has ever been, a good man; but finding it impossible to realize his own aspirations, either in religion or politics, or society, he gave up his heart to the living spirit and light within him, and avenged himself on the world by enriching it with this record of his own transcendent ideal.[6]

Coleridge knew that in interpreting Hamlet he drew an acute self-portrait. The same may be said of his response to both Milton and Wordsworth: each lived in his mind as an ideal representation of the figure within himself struggling for being. But the strength with which his mind endowed them fettered his own potential. In Milton, and increasingly in Wordsworth as his own prospects dimmed after the Nether Stowey years, he saw the figure he might have been, an ideal phantom of him- self hovering in merciless rebuke of his own inadequacies. His most salutary influence on Wordsworth was to encourage him

---

[6] *Coleridge on the Seventeenth Century*, ed. R. F. Brinkley (Dur- ham, N. C., 1955), p. 579.

in a very Coleridgean undertaking, the use of his powers to
scrutinize his own feelings and, especially in *The Prelude*, his
own mental development. But in so encouraging him, he
helped make Wordsworth into a successful version of his own
failed self. The poem he listened to at Coleorton was addressed
to himself, but in a sense it was also a poem whose authorship
he could share. But most important, in the reawakened distress
of his relationship to Wordsworth, who more and more seemed
to possess the power of Milton, Coleridge heard *The Prelude*
as an elegy for himself, an elegy he had helped shape.

"To William Wordsworth" is Coleridge's counter-elegy. It
is antiphonal to what he heard in Wordsworth's poem, conceived as though the whelmed poet was answering the verses
sung over him by his sorrowing friend. From any objective
viewpoint, his "hearing" of *The Prelude* was extravagant.
Wordsworth's intent was not, of course, to bury Coleridge.
But aspects of the poem drew from Coleridge's troubled but
deliberate egotism a responsive funeral hymn, itself shaped in
unique ways by "Lycidas."

Not that his response was purely neurotic. Wordsworth's
address to his friend occasionally sounds aloof and condescending. But the immediate impetus in *The Prelude* for Coleridge's
adaptation of the pastoral mode came from the major apostrophe to him at the end of Book Ten, the longest of a handful
of passages when "the poem to Coleridge" addresses him in
more than casual salutation.[7] The passage comes as a landing-
place in *The Prelude*, just after Wordsworth's account of his

[7] Quotations, identified by the number of the first line, are from
the "1805–6" text in *The Prelude*, ed. E. de Selincourt and H. Darbishire (Oxford, 1959). This text is de Selincourt's collation of two
manuscript copies completed by early 1806 and is the closest available approximation to the poem Coleridge heard.

own moral despair and the healing ministry at Racedown of
Coleridge and Dorothy. In late 1804, however, when Wordsworth wrote the passage, it was Coleridge who, in a crisis of
despair, had undertaken the Malta exile in search of health.
Though at Grasmere there was not much news of him—they
knew he was in Sicily briefly as a government emissary from
Malta—the Wordsworths had every reason to hope he had
found conditions for coping with addiction and recovering
health. It was much to Wordsworth's purpose to contemplate
Coleridge in Sicily, for just as his own earlier despair had come
over the degeneration of the political experiment in France, he
could imagine the similar effect of Sicily's wretched decline on
his friend,

who now,

Among the basest and the lowest fallen
Of all the race of men, dost make abode
Where Etna looketh down on Syracuse,
The City of Timoleon! Living God!
How are the Mighty prostrated! they first,
They first of all that breathe should have awaked
When the great voice was heard from out the tombs
Of ancient Heroes. If for France I have griev'd
Who, in the judgment of no few, hath been
A trifler only, in her proudest day,
Have been distress'd to think of what she once
Promised, now is, a far more sober cause
Thine eyes must see of sorrow, in a Land
Strew'd with the wreck of loftiest years, a Land
Glorious indeed, substantially renown'd
Of simple virtue once, and manly praise,
Now without one memorial hope, not even
A hope to be deferr'd; for that would serve
To chear the heart in such entire decay.                   (947)

But the land of Theocritus was also a setting appropriate to
the elegiac resolution Wordsworth wished to invoke, on the
model of "Lycidas":

> But indignation works where hope is not,
> And thou, O Friend! wilt be refresh'd. There is
> One great Society on earth,
> The noble Living and the noble Dead:
> Thy consolation shall be there, and Time
> And Nature shall before thee spread in store
> Imperishable thoughts, and the Place itself
> Be conscious of thy presence, and the dull
> Sirocco air of its degeneracy
> Turn as thou mov'st into healthful breeze
> To cherish and invigorate thy frame.
> Thine be those motions strong and sanative
> A ladder for thy Spirit to reascend
> To health and joy and pure contentedness. . . .                    (967)

Just as, in Milton's poem, the shepherd's grief modulates to a
heady vision of Lycidas's ultimate salvation, so here the poet's
lament for a Sicily weltering to the parching wind ("the dull/
Sirocco air of its degeneracy") shifts to a pleasing vision of his
friend's restoration to health through the familiar motif of the
correspondent breeze. The immortality of Lycidas, entertained
by "all the Saints above,/ In solemn troops, and sweet societies/
That sing," has a closely conceived analogue in "Imperishable
thoughts" that will console Coleridge in "the one great society
on earth," thoughts prompted by the salutary intercourse of
wretched landscape and indignant poetic consciousness.

The next lines, in which Wordsworth draws most openly on
the language of "Lycidas," turn from this putative Coleridgean
lament over Sicily to his own grief at his friend's absence from
England in troubled times. Here Milton's Angel Michael, "the

great vision of the guarded Mount," provides the model for
Wordsworth's allegorical figure of Freedom, in her English
refuge after the French debacle:

> To me the grief confined that Thou art gone
> From this last spot of earth where Freedom now
> Stands single in her only sanctuary,
> A lonely wanderer, art gone, by pain
> Compell'd and sickness, at this latter day,
> This heavy time of change for all mankind.　　　(981)

In what follows, Wordsworth invokes Coleridge's own meditative poems, "This Lime-Tree Bower My Prison" and "Frost at
Midnight," quietly superimposing their shape and gestures on
his adaptation of Miltonic elegy. Imitating the situation of
"This Lime-Tree Bower," he addresses his absent, wandering
friend, just as Coleridge in that poem addressed Charles Lamb
and the Wordsworths. Sadly alone and abandoned to his melancholy, Wordsworth finds even the *locus amoenus* of his memory, like Coleridge's Bower, without its wonted power to
cheer:

> My own delights do scarcely seem to me
> My own delights; the lordly Alps themselves,
> Those rosy Peaks, from which the Morning looks
> Abroad on many Nations, are not now
> Since thy migration and departure, Friend,
> The gladsome image in my memory
> Which they were used to be.　　　(990)

In Coleridge's earlier poem the release from the prison of dejection comes through imagined sharing of Lamb's joy in the
landscape Coleridge and the Wordsworths knew from their

walks in the Quantock Hills. That sharing culminates in an act
of blessing:

> Yes! they wander on
> In gladness all; but thou, methinks, most glad,
> My gentle-hearted Charles! for thou hast pined
> And hungered after Nature, many a year,
> In the great City pent, winning thy way
> With sad yet patient soul, through evil and pain
> And strange calamity! Ah! slowly sink
> Behind the western ridge, thou glorious Sun!
> Shine in the slant beams of the sinking orb,
> Ye purple heath-flowers! richlier burn, ye clouds!
> Live in the yellow light, ye distant groves!
> And kindle, thou blue Ocean!
>
>           ("This Lime-Tree Bower My Prison," 26–37)

Wordsworth's adaptation of this locates Coleridge in a Sicilian
landscape:

>         to kindred scenes,
> On errand, at a time how different!
> Thou tak'st thy way, carrying a heart more ripe
> For all divine enjoyment, with the soul
> Which Nature gives to Poets, now by thought
> Matur'd, and in the summer of its strength.
> Oh! wrap him in your Shades, ye Giant Woods,
> On Etna's side, and thou, O flowery Vale
> Of Enna! is there not some nook of thine,
> From the first playtime of the infant earth
> Kept sacred to restorative delight?
>
>            (996)

Then, compounding his art, he imitates the turn backward
through memory to schoolboy dreams that serves as a regen-

erative gesture for Coleridge's vexed mind in "Frost at Midnight." The turn also involves a pointed echo of "Lycidas"
("And, O ye dolphins, waft the hapless youth") and of the
moment of resurgence in "This Lime-Tree Bower" ("A de-
light/ Comes sudden on my heart"):

> Child of the mountains, among Shepherds rear'd,
> Even from my earliest school-day time, I lov'd
> To dream of Sicily; and now a strong
> And vital promise wafted from that Land
> Comes o'er my heart; there's not a single name
> Of note belonging to that honor'd isle,
> Philosopher or Bard, Empedocles,
> Or Archimedes, deep and tranquil Soul!
> That is not like a comfort to my grief. . . .          (1007)

From this roster of ancient Sicilian worthies Wordsworth
claims the solace the lime-tree bower afforded the liberated
prisoner:

> Henceforth I shall know
> That Nature ne'er deserts the wise and pure;
> No plot so narrow, be but Nature there,
> No waste so vacant, but may well employ
> Each faculty of sense, and keep the heart
> Awake to Love and Beauty!
>           ("This Lime-Tree Bower My Prison," 59–64)

Still another Sicilian analogy Wordsworth finds in the Theoc-
ritean tale of King Comates. Coleridge, imprisoned in ill health
and grief (again the parallel with "This Lime-Tree Bower"),
nevertheless, like Comates, will bring to the pastoral landscape
the poetic imagination to prevail over the circumstances of his
plight, by that grace of spirit achieving the miracle of release.

>     yea, not unmov'd
> When thinking of my own beloved Friend
> I hear thee tell how bees with honey fed
> Divine Comates, by his tyrant lord
> Within a chest imprison'd impiously
> How with their honey from the fields they came
> And fed him there, alive, from month to month,
> Because the Goatherd, blessed Man! had lips
> Wet with the Muse's Nectar.       (1016)

Finally, in reminiscence of the conclusion to "Frost at Midnight," the benevolent imagining of his friend's resurgent joy in the Sicilian beauties brightens his own spirit and culminates in a vision of Coleridge on Etna:

>     Thus I soothe
> The pensive moments by this calm fire side,
> And find a thousand fancied images
> That chear the thoughts of those I love, and mine.
> Our prayers have been accepted; Thou wilt stand
> Not as an Exile but a Visitant
> On Etna's top; by pastoral Arethuse
> Or, if that fountain be in truth no more,
> Then near some other Spring, which by the name
> Thou gratulatest, willingly deceived,
> Shalt linger as a gladsome Votary,
> And not a Captive, pining for his home.    (1028)

Released, like Lamb, from pining captivity, this Coleridge is also the theorist of the imagination Wordsworth knew, "willingly deceived" with its fictions. But Wordsworth's boldest, most unlooked-for analogy is from *Paradise Lost*. In the eleventh book, Milton describes the dazzling descent of the Archangel Michael, the "great visitant" who, in answer to Adam's prayers after the fall, with

> the heav'nly Bands
> Down from a sky of Jasper lighted now
> In Paradise, and on a Hill made alt,
> A glorious apparition. (XI, 208–11)

This final analogy, between a fully regenerate Coleridge and Milton's sublime archangel, seems an extravagant triumph of generous and amused affection. It is true that Coleridge's speculative intelligence dazzled William and Dorothy, but they were hardly inclined to allow him the total moral authority which invests Michael when he brings the vision of human history to the fallen Adam and Eve. A similar judgment can be made about the *Prelude* passage as a whole, which is "un-Wordsworthian" in style and digressive from the poem's central concerns. Agile as imitation and resourceful in analogy, it nevertheless does not go beyond deft literary pastiche, and in its failure of coalescence between playful tribute and the investment of moral power it falls short of Wordsworth's great poetic achievements in *The Prelude*. In one sense, however, Wordsworth's subtle, complex appeal to the art of Coleridge's most successful meditative poems is more than a private, friendly salute: it indicates Wordsworth's recognition of the essential compatibility of that meditative mode and the emotional structure of elegy. It was a similar fusion Coleridge sought in "To William Wordsworth."

Book Ten must have stunned Coleridge. Not only had he betrayed Wordsworth's hopes, which came now only to remind him of his continued degeneracy, but their expression in

his own meditative mode gave painful emphasis to his poetic
decline.

> For we were nursed upon the self-same hill,
> Fed the same flock, by fountain, shade, and rill.

Given the ambivalence of his emotional involvement with
Wordsworth, it is not surprising that Coleridge felt moved to
answer him in kind. What is surprising, under the circumstances, is that he could carry the elegiac motif further in a
meditative poem of more daring structural unity, in its re-
sourcefulness Coleridgean to the core. But "To William
Wordsworth" is more than a feat of literary rivalry, a casual
blending of "Lycidas" and his own meditative style. It is a
poet's attempt to move beyond the accidental personality of his
Coleorton situation to a more adequate idea of self, an assertion
of spiritual being. Prompted by Wordsworth's own inventive
echoes of "Lycidas," he found in the analogue of the drowned
poet a congenial challenge to the play of his imagination. A
year later, lecturing on drama at the Surrey Institute, he defined such imaginative play in terms which help explain the
achievement of his poem:

> One great principle is common to all [the fine arts], a prin-
> ciple which probably is the condition of all consciousness,
> without which we should feel and imagine only by discon-
> tinuous moments, and be plants or animals instead of men. I
> mean that ever-varying balance, or balancing, of images,
> notions, feelings (for I avoid the vague word, idea) con-
> ceived of as in opposition to each other; in short, the
> perception of identity and contrariety, the least degree of
> which constitutes *likeness*, the greatest absolute difference;
> but the infinite gradations between these two form all the

play and all the interest of our intellectual and moral being,
till it lead us to a feeling and an object more awful than it
seems to me compatible with even the present subject to
utter aloud, tho' I am most desirous to suggest it.[8]

With Coleridge then, in "To William Wordsworth," the play
and interest of his intellectual and moral being is in balancing
his relationship to Wordsworth with that of the two shepherd-
poets in "Lycidas." Through the mediating effect of that
analogy, Coleridge transformed his sense of personal plight into
an assertion of triumphant release in an access of reflexive
awareness.

Perhaps the chief reason why readers have treated the pastoral elegiac element in Coleridge's poem so casually is the
competing prominence of his remarkable recapitulation of *The
Prelude*. Lines eleven to forty-seven constitute an astonishingly
deft critical précis of Wordsworth's poem, elaborating its
themes in a linked series of thickly allusive clauses. At the same
time, however, Coleridge announced the analogical context of
his own undertaking with a baldly Miltonic opening:

> Theme hard as high!
> Of smiles spontaneous, and mysterious fears
> (The first-born they of Reason and twin-birth),
> Of tides obedient to external force,
> And currents self-determined, as might seem,
> Or by some inner Power; of moments awful,
> Now in thy inner life, and now abroad,
> When power streamed from thee, and thy soul received
> The light reflected, as a light bestowed—
> Of fancies fair, and milder hours of youth,

[8] *Shakespeare Criticism*, ed. T. M. Raysor (London, 1960), I,
181–82.

Hyblean murmurs of poetic thought
Industrious in its joy, in vales and glens
Native or outland, lakes and famous hills!
Or on the lonely high-road, when the stars
Were rising; or by secret mountain-streams,
The guides and the companions of thy way!
Of more than Fancy, of the Social Sense
Distending wide, and man beloved as man,
Where France in all her towns lay vibrating
Like some becalmed bark beneath the burst
Of Heaven's immediate thunder, when no cloud
Is visible, or shadow on the main,
For thou wert there, thine own brows garlanded,
Amid the tremor of a realm aglow,
Amid a mighty nation jubilant,
When from the general heart of human kind
Hope sprang forth like a full-born Deity!
—Of that dear Hope afflicted and struck down,
So summoned homeward, thenceforth calm and sure
From the dread watch-tower of man's absolute self,
With light unwaning on her eyes, to look
Far on—herself a glory to behold,
The Angel of the vision! Then (last strain)
Of Duty, chosen Laws controlling choice,
Action and joy!—An Orphic song indeed,
A song divine of high and passionate thoughts
To their own music chaunted!                         (11)

Coleridge does more here than merely summarize the argument of *The Prelude*. In his focus on the crisis of despair
sustained by Wordsworth in the aftermath of the French
Revolution, he draws an unmistakable analogy between the
calm strength achieved by Wordsworth at Racedown upon his
return to England and the strength imaginatively vested by

Milton in Michael, "the great vision of the guarded Mount."
Put another way, Coleridge, responding to Wordsworth's figure, in the passage from Book Ten, of Freedom standing
"single in her only sanctuary," found in the language of
"Lycidas" a powerful metaphor for the central theme of
Wordsworth's poem: his development, out of affliction and
despair and drawing on that experience, of an assured sense of
self. For Coleridge, such strong egotism—what he so admired
and envied in Milton and Wordsworth—was a fortress, a
"dread watch-tower." The balance of identity and contrariety
Coleridge created between the *Prelude* poet and Milton's angel
is complex. Michael, gazing south "toward Namancos and
Bayona's hold," is urged by the shepherd to "Look homeward
now"; with Coleridge, Wordsworth's sublime egotism in the
latter part of his autobiography becomes a parabolic version of
this: "summoned homeward," he is destined thenceforth "to
look/ Far on," to see (and here Coleridge is fully in touch with
Wordsworth's argument) his own self as a projected vision, a
"glory." He probably had in mind here the image of Wordsworth on Snowdon in Book Fourteen, gazing at the type of his
own intellect in the moon shining on the rifted cloudscape,
with the rising noise of waters. The careful echoes of the language of "Lycidas" (especially the "Look homeward, Angel"
strewn over five lines) constitute more than a slyly punning
code. They declare the essential link perhaps only Coleridge
among contemporary poets would have cared to declare, the
link between the sense of self and the sense of the divine, self-
knowledge being the one certain means to knowledge of God.
It is significant that Coleridge found in the language of "Lycidas" an adequate idiom for his response to Wordsworth's
achieved self-assurance. Central to his analogical purpose is his
own sense of awe toward that language. No other tribute to

Wordsworth could have cost more. Here the 1808 Surrey
Institute lecture is again helpful: for Coleridge, to ponder the
analogy between Wordsworth and Michael

> leads us to a feeling and an object more awful than it seems
> to me compatible with even the present subject to utter
> aloud, tho' I am most desirous to suggest it. For there alone
> are all things at once different and the same; there alone does
> distinction exist unaided by division—will and reason, suc-
> cession of time and unmoving eternity, infinite change and
> ineffable rest.

It is toward such a self-sufficient harmony that Coleridge heard
*The Prelude* moving:

> Then (last strain)
> Of Duty, chosen Laws controlling choice,
> Action and joy!—An Orphic song indeed,
> A song divine of high and passionate thoughts
> To their own music chaunted!                                       (43)

The abject "confession" following (quoted above, pp. 75–76)
is part, then, of the larger elegiac structure, corresponding to
the forlorn lament in "Lycidas." Wordsworth's glorious self-
sufficiency evokes despair, his Orphic song agitating the frantic
imagination of a drowning man. Under the strong sway of that
music, Coleridge becomes Lycidas, overwhelmed with con-
trasting failure and wasted gifts. But immediate and "genuine"
as the confessional seems, its pathos is mediated through the
larger design of the poem, just as the larger comic movement
of "Lycidas" leads anguish to resolution. With glances at
Milton's language pointing the chosen, controlling context,
Coleridge's abrupt turn is more cogent than the similar repudiation of "viper thoughts" in "Dejection":

That way no more! and ill beseems it me
Who came a welcomer in herald's guise
Singing of Glory and Futurity,
To wander back on such unhealthful road,
Plucking the poisons of self-harm! And ill
Such intertwine beseems triumphal wreaths
Strew'd before thy advancing!                    (76)

The impulses of rueful anxiety, leaves shattered before the
mellowing year, are rejected as self-destructive and unseemly.
Simultaneously, as with Milton's poem, counter-elegy moves
toward orthodoxy: Coleridge assumes a heraldic role for
Wordsworth's entry into a poetic Jerusalem. To retreat into
despair at his own unfulfilled promise is to refuse this higher
decorum. In Coleridge's poem, as in "Lycidas," elegiac and
Christian structure are one: the paradigm toward which the
unsettled psyche wills itself.

If one hears the isolated "confession" as the true voice of
feeling, like readers for whom the final version of "Dejection"
is at best an ambiguous triumph of art over passion, the movement beginning at line 76 will seem strained falsification on
Coleridge's part, a disavowal, in shame and defensiveness, of
the selfish jealousy of an insecure mind. Such readers will tend
to identify pathetic intensity with poetic power, and to them
there is no adequate reply beyond what Coleridge himself
might have said, that the use of a wretched despair is precisely
in providing the imagination with an occasion for release into
an ecstasy of self-awareness unavailable to a mind in steadier
equanimity. Or, as he put it to Thomas Clarkson four months
before writing the poem,

> with a certain degree of satisfaction to my own mind I can
> define the human Soul to be that class of Being, as far as we

are permitted to know, the first and lowest of the Class, which is endued with a reflex consciousness of it's own continuousness, and the great end and purpose of all it's energies & sufferings is the growth of that reflex consciousness.[9]

Put still another way, the discovery of intellectual and moral being is through pursuit of abstracted analogy. In the poem, Coleridge's release comes through the likeness discerned by the play of imagination in mediating the identity and contrariety between his reception of *The Prelude* and the fate of Lycidas.

The drowning poet's repudiation of solipsistic grief leads him to admonish his mourning friend against unseemly pity "already felt too long!" But he will not be held vindictive. "Nor let my words impart more blame than needs." As "personality" this is pusillanimous suppression of hostility for a crowned rival. But in a poem that moves beyond personality, the imputation of blame is checked less by insecure dependency on his mourner than by the willed pattern of counter-elegy, already proleptic of release. For a figure to announce that salvation Coleridge turned to the "birds of calm" from the "Ode on the Morning of Christ's Nativity": for them, in the midst of "winter wild," the tumult (like the storm in "Dejection") rose and ceased:

> for Peace is nigh
> Where Wisdom's voice has found a listening heart.
> Amid the howl of more than wintry storms,
> The Halcyon hears the voice of vernal hours
> Already on the wing.                                                    (87)

Coleridge was ready enough to discern an echo of divine creative music in authentic acts of the poetic imagination such as

[9] *Collected Letters*, II, 1197.

he heard in *The Prelude*. And the likeness implied by extending the analogy, between a Miltonic nature's sacramental response to that music and his own reaction to Wordsworth's voice, is fully consonant with the argument carefully elaborated to Clarkson. God's action on the soul of man "awakes in it a conscience of actions within itself analogous to the divine action." The ultimate, definitive divine act, that of creative self-comprehension ("I AM"), could be grasped by the human mind only through the analogy of growth in awareness of one's own "continuousness." Growth in the power of such reflection was "the first approach to, & shadow of, the divine Permanency, the first effort of the divine working in us to bind the Past and Future with the Present, and thereby to let in upon us some faint glimmering of that State in which Past, Present, and Future are co-adunated in the adorable I AM."[10] Wordsworth, like Milton's dancing Pleiades "shedding sweet influence," lets in upon Coleridge such glimmering:

> O great Bard!
> Ere yet that last strain dying awed the air,
> With steadfast eye I viewed thee in the choir
> Of ever-enduring men. The truly great
> Have all one age, and from one visible space
> Shed influence! They, both in power and act,
> Are permanent, and Time is not with them,
> Save as it worketh for them, they in it. (47)

A sense of one's continuousness—literally, a sense of past and future bound to an ontological present—is for Coleridge inconceivable "without the action of kindred souls on each other." This is the hinge of his hypothesis. It accounts for the crucial

---

[10] *Ibid.*

role of the Friend in Coleridge's meditative poems. "Man is truly altered by the coexistence of other men; his faculties cannot be developed in himself alone, & only by himself." So it takes Wordsworth to bring Coleridge to a sense of his own past and future, "in which the individual is capable of being itself contemplated as a Species of itself, namely, by its conscious continuousness moving on in an unbroken Line."[11]

But that is not all. The mediation of another fosters participation in what Coleridge called "One Life," through which "the whole Species is capable of being regarded as one individual." Transcending the limitations of the separately conceived self, lost in querulousness and melancholy, takes place not, as W. J. Bate has argued, by a "release from the burden of self-demand" that entails a diminishing of self.[12] The paradox is that "every Thing has a Life of its own, and that we are all *one Life*." If we read "To William Wordsworth" without understanding the analogies by which Coleridge projects his commitment to such a larger "Life," the poem will seem only an inventive and pathetic gesture commemorating an emotional experience. The poem argues for a mode of being that assumes a more radically Christian analysis of human life than most readers, even in Coleridge's time, would recognize. But it is because that analysis permits also the celebration of self (though at the point where self is part of a larger life) that this meditative poem, like so many others Coleridge wrote, seems to anticipate the "meditative" verse of our own day.

The last section of the poem is a lingering narrative of his pleasure in the intimate household at Coleorton, with the superadded pleasure of the recitation:

[11] *Ibid.*

[12] Walter Jackson Bate, *Coleridge* (Cambridge, Mass., 1968), p. 48.

> Eve following eve,
> Dear tranquil time, when the sweet sense of Home
> Is sweetest! moments for their own sake hailed
> And more desired, more precious, for thy song. . . .    (91)

But such simplicity is deceptive. The poem has not reverted to a merely personal, unmediated narrative. In a very Coleridgean touch, the ensuing imagery reasserts the governing pastoral analogy, with the fate of Lycidas in view, if not fully prominent view. Eight years before, on the packet boat to Germany, he had noted the appearance of the phosphorescent sea, and it may be psychologically revealing that, casting about in 1807 for imagery adequate to his meditation on spiritual death and rebirth, he turned back to his voyage with William and Dorothy (which had inaugurated an earlier release to a prosperous exile), when he

> lay in the Boat, and looked at the water, the foam of which, that beat against the Ship & coursed along by it's sides, & darted off over the Sea, was full of stars of flame.[13]

Recalling that phenomenon at Coleorton, Coleridge found a metaphor to suggest the likeness between his own response to the "various strain" of Wordsworth's poem and the motion of the drowned body of Lycidas in Milton's changing seas:

> In silence listening, like a devout child,
> My soul lay passive, by thy various strain
> Driven as in surges now beneath the stars,
> With momentary stars of my own birth,
> Fair constellated foam, still darting off
> Into the darkness; now a tranquil sea,
> Outspread and bright, yet swelling to the moon.    (95)

---

[13] *Collected Letters*, I, 425.

In *Sibylline Leaves,* as a note to the phrase "fair constellated foam," he appended a longer adaptation, first published in *The Friend,* of his original description:

> A beautiful white cloud of Foam at momently intervals coursed by the side of the Vessel with a Roar, and little stars of flame danced and sparkled and went out in it: and every now and then light detachments of this white cloud-like foam dashed off from the vessel's side, each with its own small constellation, over the Sea, and scoured out of sight like a Tartar Troop over a wilderness.

Behind this language and that of the poem is Milton's account in *Paradise Lost* of the excursions of Satan, Sin, and Death through Chaos after the fall, a passage too long to give here. These echoes in Coleridge reinforce the suggestion of the Lycidas analogy that the drowning poet's momentary plunge is into a hellish confusion,

> Where thou perhaps under the whelming tide
> Visit'st the bottom of the monstrous world.

His figure is a rich emblem. Perhaps the darting marine constellations miming the steady Wordsworthian heavens are an allusion to his own ephemeral lines in imitative response to Wordsworth's apostrophe. There are strong Platonic overtones. And it is useful to recall that he occasionally brooded over alphabetical shapes in the night skies, especially the brilliant "W" of Cassiopoeia. In notebook verses from 1807, the extremity of despair is the false starless night of a solar eclipse:

> What never is but only is to be
> This is not Life—
> O Hopeless Hope, and Death's Hypocrisy!
> And with perpetual Promise, breaks its Promises—

The Stars that wont to start, as on a chase,
And twinkling insult on Heaven's darkened Face,
Like a conven'd Conspiracy of Spies
Wink at each other with confiding eyes,
Turn from the portent, all is blank on high,
No constellations alphabet the Sky.—
The Heavens one large black Letter only shews,
And as a Child beneath its master's Blows
Shrills out at once its Task and its Affright,
The groaning World now learns to read aright,
And with its Voice of Voices cries out, O![14]

But intervening in this chaos is a mystic tranquillity, "out-spread and bright, yet swelling to the moon." The image recalls the honeydew words in the Ancient Mariner's vision:

"Still as a slave before his lord,
The ocean hath no blast;
His great bright eye most silently
Up to the Moon is cast—

If he may know which way to go;
For she guides him smooth or grim.
See, brother, see! how graciously
She looketh down on him."

Such powerful, calming grace is symbolic of the ultimate "divine action" Coleridge heard in Wordsworth's voice, the redemptive efficacy of "The dear might of him that walk'd the waves":

And when—O Friend! my comforter and guide!
Strong in thyself, and powerful to give strength!—

[14] *Notebooks*, ed. Kathleen Coburn (London, 1957–  ), Vol. II, entry no. 3107.

Thy long sustained Song finally closed,
And thy deep voice had ceased—yet thou thyself
Wert still before my eyes, and round us both
That happy vision of beloved faces—
Scarce conscious, and yet conscious of its close
I sate, my being blended in one thought
(Thought was it? or aspiration? or resolve?)
Absorbed, yet hanging still upon the sound—
And when I rose, I found myself in prayer.          (102)

In this conclusion, what at the level of personality would be blasphemy, fraught with Coleridge's problematic, self-abnegating reverence for Wordsworth, is offered instead at the level of egotism as the validation of the "One Life." Under the sway of analogy, Coleorton is Kingdom Come, where "entertain him all the Saints above,/ In solemn troops, and sweet societies/ That sing."

Wordsworth's genial apostrophe ended by investing his friend with an archangelic mantle. Coleridge's description of an ineffable intercourse following Wordsworth's recitation may return the compliment by echoing the pause after Raphael's account of creation:

The Angel ended, and in Adam's Ear
So Charming left his voice, that he a while
Thought him still speaking, still stood fixt to hear.
                                                  (VIII, 1–3)

In any case the celestial condition of mind has its analogue for Coleridge in a meditative climax, where understanding, hope, and will fuse in a resurgence of spirit tantamount to resurrection. The analogue thus recalls the gesture of Milton's uncouth swain:

At last he rose, and twitched his mantle blue:
Tomorrow to fresh woods, and pastures new.

One last speculation on the part of the poet who told his nephew that "Elegy is the form of poetry natural to the reflective mind" will help put the state toward which his poem moves in perspective as more than an occasional neurotic whim.[15] *Blackwood's* in 1821 published a selection "from Mr. Coleridge's literary correspondence" in which he urged the deliberate exertion of a meditative habit

> as a source of support and consolation in circumstances under which we might otherwise sink back on ourselves, and for want of colloquy with our thoughts, with the objects and presentations of the inner sense, lie listening to the fretful *ticking* of our sensations. . . . something is already gained, if, instead of attending to our sensations, we begin to *think* of them. But in order to this, we must reflect on these thoughts—or the same *sameness* will soon sink them down into mere feeling. And in order to sustain the act of reflection on our thoughts, we are obliged more and more to compare and generalize them, a process that to a certain extent implies, and in a still greater degree excites and introduces the act and power of abstracting the thoughts and images from their original cause, and of reflecting on them with less and less reference to the individual suffering that had been their first subject. The *vis mediatrix* of Nature is at work for us in all our faculties and habits, the associate, reproductive, comparative, and combinatory.[16]

The inclination of our age, which has witnessed the development of the art of psychoanalysis, to interest itself in confessions

[15] *Table Talk,* October 23, 1833, in *Collected Works,* VI, 491.
[16] *Collected Works,* IV, 432–33.

of anxiety more than confessions of faith has probably contributed to the emphasis which has been placed on "To William Wordsworth" as the mirror of a forlorn mind. If to us the balance in the poem between the order of art and the unshapely energy of emotion is precarious, there seems no legitimate basis for misconceiving the nature of Coleridge's undertaking or for seeing in his analogical meditation only an elaborate strategy to conceal frustration and guilt. Not disavowing but recognizing the nature of his own ambivalent aspirations after Wordsworth's power, he turned "personal" anguish into strenuous charity, and avenged himself on his friend by enriching their relationship with a poem that recorded his own egotistic and transcendent ideal. Kathleen Coburn has said that the pathos of Coleridge's problems is that he is haunted by not being able to fix an image of himself.[17] The complex analogical argument of "To William Wordsworth" posits one image of a "self" toward which he aspired most consciously and consistently. It is a thoughtful image, if an ephemeral one, and at least for the life of the poem it modifies the figure we are otherwise likely to project from dispassionate scrutiny of his personal proclivities and circumstances.

[17] "Reflections in a Coleridge Mirror: Some Images in His Poems," in *From Sensibility to Romanticism*, ed. F. W. Hilles and H. Bloom (Oxford, 1965), p. 433.

DONALD WESLING

# The Inevitable Ear:

## FREEDOM AND NECESSITY IN LYRIC FORM,

## WORDSWORTH AND AFTER

IN this paper I argue the relevance of such criteria as movement, continuity, and transition to our reading of romantic poetry. Certain writers pretend to be surprised when they find neither dazzling paradox nor purity of diction in poetry since Wordsworth. But in what follows I intend to keep implicit the demonstration that these writers have been making wrong, or at least partial, demands. The position taken is the Coleridgean one: the paper illustrates and extends Coleridge's brilliant definition of "form as proceeding" in poetry, an enterprise selected in the belief that the vexed notion of "organic

The four poems discussed in some detail in this essay are quoted from: Charles Tomlinson, *Seeing Is Believing* (London, 1960); Walt Whitman, *Leaves of Grass*, Facsimile Edition of the 1860 Text, With an Introduction by Roy Harvey Pearce (Ithaca, 1961); *The Poetical Works of William Wordsworth*, ed. Ernest de Selincourt and Helen Darbishire, 5 vols. (Oxford, 1949–58); Theodore Roethke, *The Far Field* (London, 1965).

form" has still—indeed, more than before—to be made worka-
ble, has yet to be adequately justified.

I find it necessary to begin by imagining a time that never
was, and by trusting that my description of it has some relation
to the essential history of English and American poetry since
1750. Once, then, the world was an infinitude of things, ranged
side by side. Language, in appropriating this plenitude, ges-
tured "here," then "there"; or "if," then "then"; or language
remarked "then it was that" and "now it is this." Sensation
words, image words, dominated all the mind's procedures of exposition, for the major mode of perceiving the world was that
of conjunction, addition, polarity, and analogy. Accordingly,
art was perceived as catalogue, and as "shape as superinduced."
The poem, like the mind, imitated an autonomous, external
order deployed horizontally like monuments in a field or like
those old grammar books which listed and described in isola-
tion the parts of speech, the diction as somehow separable
from the predication. Plainly, this was a bad time for poetry.

If something like this sorry state of affairs ever existed it was,
I suggest, during two periods especially in recent history: in
the period between Pope and Wordsworth, the late Augustan
time of associationism; and in the period between Whitman
and Eliot, in the early modernist time of imagism. The dis-
ability shared by Hulme, H. D., Aldington, Flint, Fletcher,
Amy Lowell, even Pound at times, with Thomson and Cowper
and the versifying topographers, is this: however superb they
may be at producing images, they have not the procedures to
coordinate them. Though imagism is a subtler, post-romantic
form of associationism, though imagist poems are not as a rule
barnacled-over with a poetic diction, the imagist poem shares
with the later Augustan poem the lack of a principle of progression. *The Seasons* is flawed from first to last by its inept
transitions, while *The Complete Poetical Works of T. E.*

*Hulme* set out systematically to suppress all transitions. Thomson like Hulme has no controlling concept, no syntax in the widest possible sense which will render perceptions fully significant.

Romantic and post-imagist poets, beginning to write in the midst of this dilemma, required a causality which would prefigure in all its transitions the effect which was the poem. The need to convert a series of perceptions into a continuous poem, and to interrelate part and whole, description and discourse, obliged them entirely to rethink the question of poetic structure. Moreover, this had to be accomplished in the process of writing poems, a task clearly more formidable for English romantic writers, involving nothing less than a total crisis of personality in the poet as in his readership. "I feel like the first men who read Wordsworth," Randall Jarrell has said in a poem: "It's so simple I can't understand it." Usually this difficult simplicity is discussed as one of diction. However, the structural *ensemble* of the continuous poem has its own unique importance: this paper will describe the structure of the continuous poem since Wordsworth and will offer, more generally, a prospectus for one sort of poetry which has strong claims to being the dominant post-romantic form.

## I

Wordsworth, Coleridge, Whitman, Wallace Stevens, William Carlos Williams, Charles Olson, Theodore Roethke all write meditative poems, in which internalized speech is designed to represent a process of thought. Perhaps rightly, critics have declined to follow the ebb and sway, the associative and dialectic structures within the sprawling, self-contradictory system of *The Prelude;* only very recently has an acute reader attempted to describe the convolutions of Stevens's "Ordinary Evening in New Haven," that "endlessly elaborating poem."[1] But the structure of shorter continuous poems, of "Tintern Abbey" or Roethke's "Meditation at Oyster River," displays a track of feeling, a motion which if followed closely will yield everything of importance for an understanding of a poet's habits of meditation. Such extended lyrics adopt the outer forms of logical discourse, advancing deliberately by devices which convey the fiction of spontaneous ordering. At best, at the same time these poems appear to be destroying form they are generating the form of a new and idiosyncratic utterance.

Even the finest of such poems have been misjudged by critics who, lacking sympathy for the romantic view of the self, have confused mere voluntariness with creative freedom. Barbara Herrnstein Smith's recent *Poetic Closure* explicitly avoids this mistake, and a beginning can be made by drawing on her findings concerning the "sense of appropriate cessation" in poetry.[2] Very likely most readers would prefer to think that the poem orders the poet's emotions, but Mrs. Smith argues the case that in the first instance the poem must be regarded as organizing the reader's emotions—that by a complex process of expectation, delay, repetition, and patterning, emotional affect is aroused, and in various kinds of good poems variously satisfied. If, as she argues, "the sense of closure is a function of the perception of structure," then Gestalt theories of the relation of part to whole and of good continuation will be useful as the critic traces the unique movement which a poem describes from its beginning to its end. Interested in poetic inevitability,

[1] See Helen Vendler, *On Extended Wings: Wallace Stevens' Longer Poems* (Cambridge, Mass., 1969).

[2] *Poetic Closure: A Study of How Poems End* (Chicago, 1968).

Mrs. Smith rightly states that "poetic structure is, in a sense, an inference which we draw from the evidence of a series of events," and that "the conclusion of a poem has special status in the process, for it is only at that point that the total pattern . . . is revealed." That the reader cannot engage the ending of a lyric without immediately engaging prosody, structure, and theme in the whole poem is her essential argument.

Such categories will be pertinent to any reading of Charles Tomlinson's "The Atlantic":

Launched into an opposing wind, hangs
    Grappled beneath the onrush,
And there, lifts, curling in spume,
    Unlocks, drops from that hold
Over and shoreward. The beach receives it,
    A whitening line, collapsing
Powdering-off down its broken length;
    Then, curded, shallow, heavy
With clustering bubbles, it nears
    In a slow sheet that must climb
Relinquishing its power, upward
    Across tilted sand. Unravelled now
And the shore, under its lucid pane,
    Clear to the sight, it is spent:
The sun rocks there, as the netted ripple
    Into whose skeins the motion threads it
Glances athwart a bed, honey-combed
    By heaving stones. Neither survives the instant
But is caught back, and leaves, like the after-image
    Released from the floor of a now different mind,
A quick gold, dyeing the uncovering beach
    With sunglaze. That which we were,
Confronted by all that we are not,
    Grasps in subservience its replenishment.

Unquestionably this is muscular yet precise. Individual offset lines are dense with perceptual content, yet very frequent *enjambement* and parallelism of syntax makes the utterance (except for the last three lines) thrust itself ahead. The first eighteen lines, describing vividly the onrush of the wave, move with authority from image to image, even extorting images from the predicates ("hangs/ Grappled"; "Powdering-off"). Only when the poem approaches its ending, with the word "like" in line nineteen, is there a failure of transition: for simile, as Charles Olson has written, "is only one bird who comes down, too easily," and here it introduces the almost separable moralizing of the last three lines, a portentous and Latinate discourse too brief to have been generated by the poem's largesse of description. Now following the Gestaltist "law of good continuation" Mrs. Smith helpfully remarks that in reading poems we expect structural principles "to continue operating as they have operated"; successful closure "allows the reader to be satisfied by the failure of continuation." On this showing, "The Atlantic" exhibits a fairly emphatic and conventional closure: but one presses on the weak ligature of the simile, and one questions whether so much energetic description can consort with so little meditation. By contrast, "Tintern Abbey" skillfully implies a successive meditation in the body of its opening description, returning glancingly to allude to that description in the far fuller context of the closing lines.

In some measure, "The Atlantic" fails to create in the reader "the expectation of nothing" and the "sense of appropriate cessation" because it does not convincingly modulate from the aesthetic to the ethical mode of thought. A poem of an earlier date, because it virtually obliterates the distinction between these modes of thought, affords one of the best instances in

literature of continuous transition. The success of this un-
metered lyric is as much as anything rhythmic and tonal:

> I saw in Louisiana a live-oak growing,
> All alone stood it, and the moss hung down from the
>     branches,
> Without any companion it grew there, uttering joyous
>     leaves of dark green,
> And its look, rude, unbending, lusty, made me think of
>     myself,
> But I wondered how it could utter joyous leaves, standing
>     alone there, without its friend, its lover near—for I
>     knew I could not,
> And I broke off a twig with a certain number of leaves
>     upon it, and twined around it a little moss,
> And brought it away—and I have placed it in sight in my
>     room,
> It is not needed to remind me as of my own dear friends,
> (For I believe lately I think of little else than of them,)
> Yet it remains to me a curious token—it makes me think of
>     manly love;
> For all that, and though the live-oak glistens there in Louisi-
>     ana, solitary, in a wide flat space,
> Uttering joyous leaves all its life, without a friend, a lover,
>     near,
> I know very well I could not.

Whitman's poem comprises one long, eddying sentence. Within
the forward thrust, different forms of delay (dash, parenthesis,
a slightly rising rhythm at line-end) deflect the poem, but not
in any unexpected way. Repetition is the major stylistic habit:
repetition of naked syntax, of clustered phrases ("uttering
joyous leaves" three times, "I knew I could not" twice), and

of sound (particularly the frequent collocation of the "th" sound and the "l" sound). By the last time the reader encounters "uttering joyous leaves," he will have come to suspect the phrase has a special meaning; presumably the tree's leaves, which are utterances, are similar to Whitman's own *Leaves of Grass*. The poem considers, but does not resolve, the question of "friendship" in the light of the solitary vocation of the poet; it makes clear that the differences between Whitman and the live-oak are as important as the similarities, and since there is no possible resolution the ending is highly tentative.

This is not, then, the kind of poem W. B. Yeats admired, which would click when it ended like the lid of a box. The effect is of *coming round*, rather than of closing, though of course conventional elements of modulation-toward-closure are present in the summary quality of the "and though" phrase in the third-to-last line, and in the intensifying addition of "very well" to the earlier "I knew I could not," in the brief concluding line. As a dialectical testing of similarities and differences of the sort described above, the poem illustrates Mrs. Smith's contention that "as one moves from more to less highly determined forms, closural effects become increasingly dependent upon thematic structure and special non-structural devices." In the absence of received rhyme-schemes, stanzaic structures, and meters, which are of course supplanted here by syntax as the primary indication of structure, the rhythms of such poems are to be understood only by case-law: by scrutiny of the system of conventions that each poem invents for itself. The poet who adopts such an innovating metric takes risks: other poems by Whitman and by poets in his tradition will not prove so tightly self-sufficient as the live-oak poem. However, if the reader regards this poem as woolly, redundant, and diffuse, he is unwilling to enjoy—much less to define and discriminate—the pleasures of what Northrop Frye has aptly termed "diffusion of sense" in poetry.


II


Poets in any given period will usually differ greatly in the degree to which they crave the authority of received poetic forms. Yet it does seem generally true that poetry has moved from a highly determinate period style in the age of Pope (heroic couplet, enclosed quatrain, epigram, and maximal closure) to a hazardous but salutary freedom in the modern age (blank verse, free verse, the concrete poem, and minimal closure). Again, in an acute period of crisis and redefinition for ordinary language and ordinary logic, such as the late eighteenth and early twentieth centuries, the related question of poetic structure will also be profoundly vexed. Earl Wasserman has remarked how especially revealing it is that the one "organizing scheme the later eighteenth century developed, and the one from which it drew its greatest sense of meaningful order, was associationism." "The substitution of infinite diversity for *concordia discors* as a controlling concept resulted in merely versified catalogues" and in what Wasserman calls "the bifurcated descriptive-moral poem" of the later eighteenth century. He goes on: "The syntax of the description remains distinct from the syntax of the moralizing, and the failure to bring them together is the failure to generate a new syntax, without which there is no poem, and no need for one."[3] That is a situation very similar to the one enunciated by those des-

[3] See Chapter V, *The Subtler Language* (Baltimore, 1959).

perate fragments called "Cinders" and placed toward the end of Hulme's *Speculations;* and "clear cut images," in Aldington's phrase, or the image defined as "an emotional and intellectual complex in an instant of time" (Pound), seem calculated deliberately to evade the connective powers of the mind.

Ezra Pound, Louis Zukofsky, and Robert Creeley would appear to be imagists searching for the measure, the proper discourse. The same might be said of the early Coleridge, before the discovery of a continuous "Conversation" poem coincided in his career with his abandonment of mechanistic systems of philosophy; or of Wordsworth before 1798. Since the question—of how to get from image to discourse, or more broadly of how to express a significant apprehension of the world—is preeminently one of method, we are fortunate to have two remarkable texts to rely on. Here is Dr. Johnson, commenting in the "Life of Thomson" on the structure of Thomson's *Seasons:*

> The great defect of *The Seasons* is want of method; but for this I know not that there was any remedy. Of many appearances subsisting all at once, no rule can be given why one should be mentioned before another; yet the memory wants the help of order, and the curiosity is not excited by suspense or expectation.

This is very likely unanswerable as an analysis of why it is that whole poems will not come of the attempt to build up a world by versified catalogue. Nevertheless, for Johnson a poem is still to be regarded as a reflection or imitation of an autonomous order outside itself; he cannot conceive any remedy for "want of method."

We are taken further by the second text, Coleridge's brilliant treatise "On Method." Here Coleridge asks how we distinguish, even among educated men, "the man of superior mind"; and he answers:

> It is the unpremeditated and evidently habitual arrangement of his words, grounded on the habit of foreseeing, in each integral part, or (more plainly) in every sentence, the whole that he then intends to communicate. However irregular and desultory his talk, there is method in the fragments.

If "absence of method" is occasioned by "an habitual submission of the understanding to mere events and images as such," method on the other hand "becomes natural to the mind which has been accustomed to contemplate not things only, or for their own sake, but likewise and chiefly the relations of things, either their relations to each other, or to the observer, or to the state and apprehension of the hearers." Method thus consists of a striving after genuine relationships. The excellence of Shakespeare's art, for instance, consists in a "just proportion," a "union and interpenetration . . . of the universal and the particular." So much might be expected from any romantic theorist, but what follows on this could only have come from a man habitually obsessed by what he called "the streamy nature of association":

> For method implies a progressive transition, and it is the meaning of the word in the original language. The Greek μέθοδος is literally a way or path of transit. . . . As without continuous transition there can be no method, so without a preconception there can be no transition with continuity. The term, method, cannot therefore, otherwise than by abuse, be applied to a mere dead arrangement, containing in itself no principle of progression.

There is a closely related sentence in the essay "On Poesy or Art":

> Remember that there is a difference between form as pro-
> ceeding, and shape as superinduced;—the latter is either the
> death or the imprisonment of the thing;—the former is its
> self-witnessing and self-effected sphere of agency.

Method as "progressive transition" and form "as proceeding"
are the operative definitions, but it is also essential to take the
force of concepts such as "relation" and "preconception"—so
as to be very clear that the process Coleridge describes is not
uncontrolled but the graph of a particular sort of intellection.

More exactly what sort may be suggested by noting that
Wordsworth, in "Tintern Abbey," manages to avoid the way-
ward construction of *The Seasons*—a poem similar in descrip-
tive-meditative intent—by arranging the gradual revelation of
a discovery and by moving steadily deeper into his subject. It
emerged from examining poems by Whitman and Tomlinson
that there is, in a number of romantic and post-romantic
poems, a tendency toward diffusion rather than concentration
of sense: a style which, subsuming image by discourse, employs
the phenomenon of repetition in a special way. Progressive
transition in such poetry will require the design of continuity
by a sequential shuttling from image to idea and from idea to
image, at best an interpenetration of thing and thought.

"Tintern Abbey" opens with twenty-two lines of description. The outer landscape, a store of images important in itself
and as a reminder of the Wordsworth who visited the Wye
Valley five years before, is observed yet curiously transparent.
The details of cliffs and valley, cottages, orchards, woodlands,
"wreaths of smoke," perhaps especially the unseen imagined
Hermit who poetlike "sits alone," are all wonderfully noticed,
yet they are also phenomena of the mind and images of rural
meditation. The steep protective cliffs "impress" on the "wild
secluded scene . . ./ Thoughts of more deep seclusion," and

those thoughts are the poem itself. So secluded is the scene that the smoke wreaths which imply human presence ascend undispersed "in silence, from among the trees." It is this emphasis on seclusion as the precondition of mature human thought, inseparable from the opening lines of apparent description, which unites the opening of the poem with the solemn thinking which follows. With what Coleridge called "the rapidity necessary to Pathos," it prepares the effortless transition to another phase of the subject, the notions of absence and ecstasy in the second verse-paragraph. By a masterful act of premeditation, imagination presents the whole poem in the opposition of exposure and seclusion, absence and return, in the opening landscape.

The tentative, exploratory thinking in the body of "Tintern Abbey" moves through a process of intellection which deepens the reference of the opening description, and thus the poem becomes the perfect flowering of the loco-descriptive genre. The distinction of Wordsworth is that at best landscape is inseparable from such sequences of generalization. "There is also a meditative, as well as a human, pathos," he said, "an enthusiastic, as well as an ordinary, sorrow; a sadness that has its seat in the depths of reason, to which the mind cannot sink gently of itself—but to which it must descend by treading the steps of thought."[4] Here is a passage from the heart of the poem in the central meditative style:

> And now, with gleams of half-extinguished thought,
> With many recognitions dim and faint,
> And somewhat of a sad perplexity,
> The picture of the mind revives again:
> While here I stand, not only with the sense
> Of present pleasure, but with pleasing thoughts

[4] *Poetical Works*, II, 428.

That in this moment there is life and food
For future years. And so I dare to hope,
Though changed, no doubt, from what I was when first
I came among these hills; when like a roe
I bounded o'er the mountains, by the sides
Of the deep rivers, and the lonely streams,
Wherever nature led: more like a man
Flying from something that he dreads than one
Who sought the thing he loved. For nature then
(The coarser pleasures of my boyish days,
And their glad animal movements all gone by)
To me was all in all.—I cannot paint
What then I was. The sounding cataract
Haunted me like a passion: the tall rock,
The mountain, and the deep and gloomy wood,
Their colours and their forms, were then to me
An appetite; a feeling and a love,
That had no need of a remoter charm,
By thought supplied, nor any interest
Unborrowed from the eye.

Here is a mind almost entirely in possession of its experience. The noble and declarative language moves with tough intent toward the actualizing of that experience and the discovery of its personal meaning and use. The style might be called excursive or generative: clauses are linked by association, and sentences carry the discourse further by a simple "And so," or "for"; indeed the connective "and" is worked hard, as is the amplifying "not only . . . but" construction. The back-and-forth movement from past to present time, the intrusive present consciousness qualifying nostalgia at every point as soon as it is expressed, the very convolutions of tense, reenact the processes of a mind in the throes of self-definition.

Wordsworth continues:

> —That time is past,
> And all its aching joys are now no more,
> And all its dizzy raptures. Not for this
> Faint I, nor mourn nor murmur; other gifts
> Have followed; for such loss, I would believe,
> Abundant recompense. For I have learned
> To look on nature, not as in the hour
> Of thoughtless youth; but hearing oftentimes
> The still, sad music of humanity,
> Nor harsh nor grating, though of ample power
> To chasten and subdue. And I have felt
> A presence that disturbs me with the joy
> Of elevated thoughts; a sense sublime
> Of something far more deeply interfused,
> Whose dwelling is the light of setting suns,
> And the round ocean and the living air,
> And the blue sky, and in the mind of man:
> A motion and a spirit, that impels
> All thinking things, all objects of all thought,
> And rolls through all things. Therefore am I still
> A lover of the meadows and the woods,
> And mountains; and of all that we behold
> From this green earth; of all the mighty world
> Of eye, and ear,—both what they half create,
> And what perceive; well pleased to recognise
> In nature and the language of the sense
> The anchor of my purest thoughts, the nurse,
> The guide, the guardian of my heart and soul
> Of all my moral being.

The reader is convinced, carried onward by the authenticity of such a mind when it is so engaged, and he comes to know what Wordsworth means in saying the purpose of the poems "is to follow the fluxes and refluxes of the mind when agi-

tated by the great and simple affections of our nature." Since
in this kind of writing even "repetition and apparent tautology
are frequent beauties of the highest kind," "Tintern Abbey"
(a "highly imaginative" poem, unlike the ones he called "simply human") is in conception allowably disheveled, tautologi-
cal, irregular.[5] Although Wordsworth makes a show of ratioci-
nation, it can hardly be said that he is here following the steps
of an argument. Rather, his method is to exhibit the complete
movement of a full mind which has found a pretext for stock-
taking, a mapping of the self with relation to a significant
landscape.

On the level of the line, the meditative style is amplifying,
incremental. Wordsworth's strength is that of plain syntax,
meaning draped over the ends of lines, sometimes pulled up
short at line-end; or backtracking, eliding past punctuation
marks, creating and destroying balance in the phrasing. Par-
alellism (as in: "with gleams . . . with many recognitions"),
apposition, digressive delay, inversion (as in: "recognitions
dim"), parataxis, polysyndeton (as in: "And the round ocean
and the living air,/ And the blue sky"), negative affirmation
(as in: "nor any interest/ Unborrowed from the eye")—the
list covers only a few of the major elements of a discourse
which rarely lets thought cling to a metaphor, preferring to
"spread" it by extension of syntax. For instance, in the final
ten-line sentence in the last-quoted passage, a masterful use of
the connective "and" keeps syntax lucid, telescoping or ex-
panding the sense as required, contributing to the density of
"both what they half create,/ And what perceive."

The use of the transitional (but not strictly logical) "There-

[5] *Ibid.*, pp. 388*n*, 513; and *The Letters of William and Dorothy
Wordsworth: The Middle Years*, ed. Ernest de Selincourt, 2 vols.
(Oxford, 1937), I, 128.

fore" is one of the stylistic habits of the poem as a whole—
as is the bold dash, the intensifying "all" and "purest," and
the catalogue whose members ascend in significance. One catalogue has the device which may be called "faulty series":

> something far more deeply interfused,
> Whose dwelling is the light of setting suns,
> And the round ocean and the living air,
> And the blue sky, and in the mind of man. . . .

The preposition "in" complicates the progression, bearing as
it does the full weight of Wordsworthian pondering on mind
and world. The calculated vagueness of "something" may
seem an evasion, like the anxious circumlocution near the end
of the poem, "If I should be where I no more can hear/ Thy
voice," where Wordsworth seems to imply his death. It seems
likely that he uses vagueness or periphrasis to get over gaps,
to touch only lightly on matters about which he is uncertain.
Occasionally he gives an honest admission—"I cannot paint/
What then I was"—which aids the illusion of spontaneity: the
poem as the act of the mind, finding its own materials, brood-
ing on its habitual associations, admitting limits.

Wordsworth hoped "that in the transitions, and the impassioned music of the versification" would be found the impet-
uosity he thought characteristic of the Ode form.[6] That is
why he thrust the sense from caesura to caesura, affording a
speed and suppleness which the blank verse of Akenside or
Young—trapped in Miltonic rhythms—could not manage. And
that is why he selected and transmuted his details with delicate
concern, attended to transitions, and deepened key words in
their contexts. Nevertheless, a poem which has derived from

[6] *Poetical Works,* II, 517.

a complex, unsettling perception of the difference between a changing self and an unchanging landscape must also throw up resistances. Carried along the forward motion will be contradictory elements of the sort that are united in actual experience but dissolve upon merely logical inspection. The "mysticism" of the poem (as in: "We see into the life of things") corrects itself by inclusion of specifics; orotund abstraction, by description or the plain style (as in: "That best portion of a good man's life"); and the inward preoccupation of the adult mind, by continual acknowledgment of the educative value of landscape. Meditative style thus reinforces the poem's intent of weighing the "aching joys" of "thoughtless youth" against an adult's consciousness which is no longer naïve about perception. If it did not, Keats would not have called "Tintern Abbey," a proof Wordsworth could "think into the human heart," a poem with no attained "balance of good and evil" yet "explorative of those dark passages" of responsible life reached at the brink of maturity.[7] Such exploration is prosodic as well as personal, a way of making "impassioned music" from the discursive and naked language of the thinking mind.

## III

One of the finest moments in the *Biographia Literaria* occurs when Coleridge, discussing in Chapter 12 the assertion by Hobbes and Hartley "that all real knowledge supposes a prior sensation," transcends their associationism with an astonishing

[7] *Letters*, ed. H. E. Rollins (Cambridge, Mass., 1958), I, 280–81.

sentence: "For sensation itself is but vision nascent, not the cause of intelligence, but intelligence itself revealed as an earlier power in the process of self-construction." This conviction, that "sensation is . . . intelligence itself," is shared by Wordsworth, author of a whole body of poems on the growth of his own mind, and of some notable lines which ascribe his own most cherished identity to his seagoing brother John, who "from the solitude/ Of the vast sea" is said to have brought

> a watchful heart
> Still couchant, an inevitable ear,
> And an eye practiced like a blind man's touch.
> ("When, to the attractions of the busy world")

Because John's sensation is nascent vision, Wordsworth can conflate poetic intelligence into general human intelligence to call him "A *silent* Poet." Watchful heart, inevitable ear, tactile eye: the sequence places the executive and human skills of the ear before those of the eye, suggesting the priority, in time and importance, of what T. S. Eliot has called the auditory imagination.

Charles Olson advances virtually the same point of view in "Projective Verse" (1950), an essay which praises the writer who can "put himself in the open," composing verse "as though not the eye but the ear was to be its measurer," "the ear, which is so close to the mind that it is the mind's, that it has the mind's speed."[8] When Olson asks "the sons of Pound and Williams" to support "the revolution of the ear, 1910, the trochee's heave," his position is not, after all, so far from that of a poet who thought meter a "superadded beauty" which

[8] *Selected Writings*, ed. Robert Creeley (New York, 1966).

was "but adventitious to composition" (as Wordsworth has it in the 1802 Appendix to the Preface of *Lyrical Ballads*). Olson's mention of Pound and 1910 raises once again the question of Imagism, a movement which won a nonmetrical verse at the price of its dominance by the outward eye. Fortunately the early poems of Eliot and the first of Pound's *Cantos* deepened and enriched Imagist prosodies, subsuming them by processes of thought and releasing free rhythms for new uses either separately or in counterpoint with traditional meters. Thus, while the ocular intelligence has since 1910 produced countless notational poems, Haiku in English, and more recently concrete poems, most of them incorrigibly minor because they evade the necessity of discourse, a concurrent poetics of the inevitable ear in such writers as Stevens, Williams, and Roethke has given us a collection of writing (to borrow a phrase from Wordsworth's 1800 Preface) "important in the multiplicity and quality of its moral relations."

Roethke's "Meditation at Oyster River" is a distinguished example of a recent continuous poem. The first of its four sections is all but prolix with the Wordsworthian need to specify place and time. The lines are tentacular, hesitant:

> Over the low, barnacled, elephant-colored rocks,
> Come the first tide-ripples, moving, almost without sound,
>     toward me,
> Running along the narrow furrows of the shore, the rows
>     of dead clam shells;
> Then a runnel behind me, creeping closer,
> Alive with tiny striped fish, and young crabs climbing in
>     and out of the water.

This section, like the ensuing three, ends descriptively:

A fish raven turns on its perch (a dead tree in the river-
mouth),
Its wings catching a last glint of the reflected sunlight.

Roethke leaps from this to the desperate opening lines of the
second section:

The self persists like a dying star,
In sleep, afraid. Death's face rises afresh. . . .

If this is to be seen as a major transition and not as a crippling
break in the poem's structure, it is necessary to inquire more
carefully into the nature of the scene, at twilight by the mouth
of an estuarial river, with "No sound from the bay. No violence," and with the tide rising "almost without sound." It
appears that the tidal recurrence of gentle and violent waters,
of safety and danger, is the mind's cycle as well, reenacted in
the process of the poem. Roethke's meditation carries along
resistances more explicitly than Wordsworth's, re-creating a
swing from mood to mood rather than attempting to demon-
strate an achieved stability.

Especially in the first and last sections, the dominant mood
is calm. Yet even here the absence of violence has itself to be
registered. The scene is so described as first to imply and then
to call up its contrary, while the speaker draws out the personal significance of his opening description. The climax occurs
in section three, not as outward noticing but as remembered
violence in the waters of a distant river,

the Tittebawassee, in the time between winter and spring,
When the ice melts along the edges in early afternoon.
And the midchannel begins cracking and heaving from the
pressure beneath,

> The ice piling high against the iron-bound spiles,
> Gleaming, freezing hard again, creaking at midnight—

And at this point the speaker turns from memory to a present wish:

> And I long for the blast of dynamite,
> The sudden sucking roar as the culvert loosens its debris of
>     branches and sticks,
> Welter of tin cans, pails, old bird nests, a child's shoe riding
>     a log,
> As the piled ice breaks away from the battered spiles,
> And the whole river begins to move forward, its bridges
>     shaking.

In another of Roethke's last poems, "The Abyss," the desire to dream "beyond this life" and to "outleap the sea" is voiced more nakedly, but here it finds oblique expression in the images —at once psychological and objective—of a "pressure beneath" and a "blast of dynamite." Fearing death and needing it, self-frozen and self-frightened, the self invokes violent release into the unconsciousness of water or of the lower forms of life:

> Death's face rises afresh,
> Among the shy beasts, the deer at the salt-lick,
> The doe with its sloped shoulders loping across the highway,
> The young snake, poised in green leaves, waiting for its fly,
> The hummingbird, whirring from quince-blossom to
>                     morning-glory—
> With these I would be.

By a delicate and deliberate use of pathetic fallacy with respect to beasts and waters, self-destructiveness is suffused into the particulars of the scene. Yet the poem's careful rhythms contain and objectify its desperation. Limber and inevitable lines such as

The doe with its sloped shoulders loping across the highway,

and

The ice piling high against the iron-bound spiles,

are typical of a discourse which uses a descriptive vocabulary to express an intense inwardness, and they are anything but unmeasured and inexact.

Having come further than Wordsworth in a fascination with dissolving identities, Roethke longs to experience the pre-history of consciousness itself: "Water's my will, and my way," he says in the final section. The same is true for others since Wordsworth who employ successfully the fluid yet weighty medium of an innovating metric. In conceiving of the mind as in large measure self-destroying, but also in large measure self-creating, the psychology and prosody of the in-evitable ear are at one. The tendency toward the dissolution of personal identity and the weakening of poetic shape will always exist in such a scheme, but as a risk which imposes a responsibility. Accordingly Lawrence, Pound, and Williams, admiring Whitman but believing he took the principle of dif-fusion of sense too far, refine his inheritance by seeking more craftsmanly dynamics in the line and in the poem as a whole. "Freedom, was what [Whitman] understood. That alone," said Williams:

But Freedom cannot be the end of it. . . . No verse can be free. That is solely a confusion in terms: all verse must be measured, The sole problem [*sic*] where shall we find the measure?[9]

Perhaps the measure will be found by some extension of Williams's own concept of "the variable foot," perhaps by one of the sons of Olson going "down through the workings of his own throat to the place where breath comes from" (as Olson asks in "Projective Verse"); but it is more likely that it is the nature of this measure to be elusive, requiring that each poetic utterance authenticate its form as it proceeds. That, I take it, is what Emerson meant when he demanded a "meter-making argument": not unlicensed freedom, but the persistent invention of new forms of necessity.

[9] "Measure," *Spectrum* (Santa Barbara, Fall, 1959).

WILLIAM H. PRITCHARD

# Wildness of Logic

# in Modern Lyric

MY title is lifted from Robert Frost's essay "The Figure a Poem Makes," a four-page mine of striking formulations put just as clearly, or obscurely, as was Frost's habit. At the outset a statement of belief—or is it fact?—is made:

> The possibilities for tune from the dramatic tones of meaning struck across the rigidity of a limited meter are endless. And we are back in poetry as merely one more art of having something to say, sound or unsound. Probably better if sound, because deeper and from wider experience.

The useful pun boldly yokes together, declares inseparable, the "soundness" of a poem's view of things and the way it carries itself to our ear as we move through it; further, Frost asserts that tones of meaning struck against the rigidity of meter are best sounded, most *sound*, because they come most strongly connected with life—"deeper and from wider experience." He then proceeds to introduce the term I have appropriated:

Then there is this wildness whereof it is spoken. Granted
again that it has an equal claim with sound to being a poem's
better half. If it is a wild tune, it is a poem. Our problem
then is, as modern abstractionists, to have the wildness pure;
to be wild with nothing to be wild about. We bring up as
aberrationists, giving way to undirected associations and
kicking ourselves from one chance suggestion to another in
all directions as of a hot afternoon in the life of a grass-
hopper. Theme alone can steady us down. Just as the first
mystery was how a poem could have a tune in such a
straightness as meter, so the second mystery is how a poem
can have wildness and at the same time a subject that shall
be fulfilled.

And a bit further on:

I tell how there may be a better wildness of logic than of
inconsequence. But the logic is backward, in retrospect,
after the act. It must be more felt than seen ahead like
prophecy. It must be a revelation, or a series of revelations,
as much for the poet as for the reader.

A reviewer in the *TLS* recently wagged his finger at Santayana for not communicating his thought clearly and directly.
No doubt Frost could be also so censured: "Then there is this
wildness whereof it is spoken. . . ." Which wildness? Spoken
of by whom? Whereof? Why doesn't he tell us his meaning
in plain words? It seems that, at the very least, Santayana and
Frost are more playful writers than the *TLS* reviewer; when
it came time for Frost to write about what a poem was he
found that clear and direct communication of thoughts wasn't
quite what he had in mind. In the closing words from one of
his poems:

I could give all to Time except—except
What I myself have held. But why declare

The things forbidden that while the Customs slept
I have crossed to Safety with? For I am There,
And what I would not part with I have kept.

By analogy, the mysteries of how a poem has tune in the
straightness of meter, or wildness in the fulfilled subject—the
"logic"—these mysteries are not to be declared so that we can
copy them down and take them to heart. They are to be
smuggled across instead by the figures poems make.

It might be argued that Frost's demands on poetry are no
more than temperamental hints; clever ways of publicizing his
own brand of new verse; forceful attempts at exhortation or
self-justification masquerading as statements of fact. But to
understand and perhaps write them off in this way may be
too easy: one more bland historical act of placing and therefore distancing somebody else's words, performed at no cost
and little value to ourselves. My interest is, rather, in the extent to which some American poets since Frost have taken him
to heart and behaved in their poems as if his demands must
be heeded. Beyond that, in whether these demands have any
implications for ways a reader, a teacher, a critic, should respond in the face of contemporary poems whose status in the
ideal order of poetry isn't fixed, and which may therefore be
approached relatively unencumbered with critical-historical
luggage. Emerson claimed he knew how to behave perfectly
in the face of the new poems of his contemporaries: "I see
in a moment, on looking into our new *Dial*, which is the wild
poetry, and which the tame, and see that one wild line out of
a private heart saves the whole book." Over a century later
we are still looking for and demanding wild lines out of private hearts; yet surrounded by poets who assure us that they
will bare their private heart, soul, and if possible body to us,

we may wonder whether Emerson's or Frost's promotion of wildness isn't by now superfluous.


I


Reference to Frost's own poetic wildness should surprise no one. At the poet's eighty-fifth birthday celebration in 1959 Lionel Trilling saluted him as an authentic tragic writer comparable to Sophocles, at which point the Dark Frost (actually discovered some years before by Randall Jarrell) leaped into prominence, and one was admonished to look out for poems in which bleak views of nature and human nature prevailed. (You may have thought, the argument ran, that he was just going on about cows and trees in New England, but underneath it all things were really grim and pessimistic.) It was only too easy to domesticate the Dark Frost: the right poems to quote were "Design," "Desert Places," "The Most of It," "Neither Out Far Nor In Deep," or "Acquainted with the Night," and as long as critical discourse was conducted in terms of "the poet's attitude toward the cosmos, or existence, or nature, or man . . ." the discourser could go blithely on his way, taming supposedly wild utterances into an illustration of his favorite concept. But it should be remembered that Frost uses "wild" to modify "tune"—"if it is a wild tune, it is a poem"—thus suggesting that talk about wildness must be talk about how the voice of a poem sounds: "We must imagine the speaking voice," he says over and over in his letters; "never if you can help it write down a sentence in which the voice will not know how to posture specially."

Suppose we confront the reader of a poem with these directives and let him improvise a bit: "We must imagine . . . I must imagine the speaking voice, and yet at this particular spot in the poem I'm not quite sure exactly how it should sound . . ." Or perhaps, "Yes, I see that this sentence demands a special posture, it's no run-of-the-mill utterance, and I've more or less got it, I think, although . . ." Moments like these, inadequately designated by ellipsis, occur often in a reader's life—unusually often, when reading Frost; and they should be handled with a good portion of negative capability in order to preserve them from being neatly ironed out into The Right Reading. What is to be said, for example, in response to "Never Again Would Birds' Song Be the Same"?

He would declare and could himself believe
That the birds there in all the garden round
From having heard the daylong voice of Eve
Had added to their own an oversound,
Her tone of meaning but without the words.
Admittedly an eloquence so soft
Could only have had an influence on birds
When call or laughter carried it aloft.
Be that as may be, she was in their song.
Moreover her voice upon their voices crossed
Had now persisted in the woods so long
That probably it never would be lost.
Never again would birds' song be the same.
And to do that to birds was why she came.

The poem is about Eve, about love, about the persistence of song; the difficult thing to pin down is just how it's about them. What are the correct words to chart a medium through which the speaking voice moves by connectives like "Admittedly," "Could only," "Be that as may be," "Moreover," and "probably"? Unassertive? Quietly certain? Who is the brave man willing to stake his reputation on identifying the tone of voice at a particular moment of this eloquence so soft? We must imagine the speaking voice, yes: but doesn't the wildness of this tune—for all its "tame" subject matter—leave us pretty much speechless? Convinced we have heard a very specially posturing voice indeed, we are ready to admire it, delight in its mastery, yet not so ready to say just what it is we admire it *as*, delight in it *for*. To paraphrase Randall Jarrell's paraphrase of St. Augustine on time: "We know what this poem is about, we know how it sounds, just so long as you don't ask us to say exactly." Perhaps the "possibilities for tune" Frost speaks of in his essay have little to do with the attempt to communicate thoughts clearly and directly; perhaps the wild poem is a performance, a play of mind and ear a little beyond us and scarcely abiding our questions about it.

To do that to words was why he came: Frost does it also in poems where one would least expect to find it—in the relatively didactic, witty sermonizing he became increasingly fond of, to the despair of those partisans of the Dark Frost. Nothing seemingly could be further from lyric wildness than the cadences of "Departmental" or "Why Wait for Science," or at first glance a poem titled "The Lost Follower":

As I have known them passionate and fine,
The gold for which they leave the golden line
Of lyric is a golden light divine,
Never the gold of darkness from a mine.

The spirit plays us strange religious pranks
To whatsoever god we owe the thanks.

No one has ever failed the poet ranks
To link a chain of money-metal banks.

The loss to song, the danger of defection
Is always in the opposite direction.
Some turn in sheer, in Shelleyan dejection
To try if one more popular election

Will give us by shortcut the final stage
That poetry with all its golden rage
For beauty on the illuminated page
Has failed to bring—I mean the Golden Age.

And if this may not be (and nothing's sure),
At least to live ungolden with the poor,
Enduring what the ungolden must endure.
This has been poetry's great anti-lure.

The muse mourns one who went to his retreat
Long since in some abysmal city street,
The bride who shared the crust he broke to eat
As grave as he about the world's defeat.

With such it has proved dangerous as friend
Even in a playful moment to contend
That the millennium to which you bend
In longing is not at a progress-end

By grace of state-manipulated pelf,
Or politics of Ghibelline or Guelph,
But right beside you book-like on a shelf,
Or even better god-like in yourself.

He trusts my love too well to deign reply.
But there is in the sadness of his eye,
Something about a kingdom in the sky
(As yet unbrought to earth) he means to try.

For all its sheer, its Frostian cleverness, for all its selection of a particularly unyielding net to play tennis over (the loud clomping end rhymes, four to a stanza), the poem is something more and something more remote from us than, say, the cozily knowing "Departmental," a clever but tame poem. It is in the first line of the final stanza where that "more" is revealed, coming as it does after a preceding sentence of eight lines which has its undeviable say in a godlike voice ("That the millennium to which you bend . . . is . . . right beside you book-like on a shelf,/ Or even better god-like in yourself"). Suddenly an even, virtually monosyllabic declaration:

He trusts my love too well to deign reply.

What is declared here? How much dignity does the trusting "he" possess? He is right to trust the poet's love, surely. It is right that he not "deign" to reply, but it is also amusing—after all he's got his mind on higher things, "Something about a kingdom in the sky." Who is condescending to whom, exactly? We could ask more questions and decide that the line is a mixture of affection, superiority, firmness about somebody's intractable otherness, wistful regret that such is the case. And wherever we came out the voice would still remain a little beyond our characterizing words, refusing to reveal to us its special posture. As with "Never Again Would Birds' Song Be the Same" the poem at this playful moment is a wild tune; its play not of the vulgar tongue-in-cheek sort Frost too often invoked when he spoke self-satisfiedly of "my kind of fooling," but a less willful and manipulated, a stranger and wilder kind of play. Such moments when they occur lift a relaxed professional exercise like "The Lost Follower" into a higher lyric reach, transforming "logic" into something else.

II

In an essay titled "Sincerity and Poetry"[1] Donald Davie has argued that the tide of confessional poetry in the 1960s (the publication of Lowell's *Life Studies* having opened the flood-gates) has forced us to reexamine and readjust our notions about the impersonality of poems, how they are separate from the man who wrote them and how it is foolish or irrelevant to apply a criterion of "sincerity" to what is merely words on the page used well. His most pertinent remarks occur as he advises us how to behave in relation to the poems of our con-temporaries: we need not dismantle all our Eliotic and new-critical assumptions about impersonality since

> In part, at least, the measure of a poet's sincerity is, it must be, *inside his poem*. This is to say that confessional or pro-phetic pretensions in the poet do not absolve him from pro-ducing poems that are well-written.

But Davie goes on to say that we must learn to look upon "ambiguity"—"a high incidence of words with double mean-ings"—as a feature of only *one* kind of good poetry, not all kinds. And he continues:

> For different reasons, irony and paradox are features which we must learn to set less store by. We must learn . . . to give more weight to other features, notably to the *tone* in which the poet addresses us, and to the fall and pause and

[1] Donald Davie, "Sincerity and Poetry," *Michigan Quarterly Re-view* (Winter, 1966), p. 7.

run of spoken American or spoken English as the poet plays it off against his stanza-breaks and line-divisions. In short a poet can control his poem in many more ways, or his control of it manifests itself in more ways, than until lately we were aware of.

It is not clear to whom this "we" refers, since the evidence is that Frost, for one, was fully aware of the possibilities for such control—such a tune—at least as early as 1913. Nor is this control (which Davie eventually calls "sincerity") something we suddenly began to look for and demand in poems during the last ten years. Anyone impressed by Frost's remarks about poetry would welcome Davie's suggestion that we learn to give more weight to the "tone in which the poet addresses us"; though, as the examples from Frost's poems show, giving weight to "the tone" can be a problematic and fascinating matter when reading an ambiguous poet.

It should be emphasized, however, that there is plenty of identifiable tone in Frost's poetry, against which the wild, playful, not-quite identifiable moments considered earlier can stand out. In looking at some poems and moments from six-ties poems the problems of how one gives weight to the tone are frequently of a different sort. For example, what if the tone of a contemporary poem is monolithic monotone, monotonous in its prophetic solemnity? In a postscript to his anthology *A Controversy of Poets* Robert Kelly has attacked "academic verse" as "social decorative verse which serves to reinforce the typical attitudes of its presumed readers" and is a betrayal of poetry's true function, since the academic poet chooses to write in "time-worn, pre-existent patterns . . . often enough in outworn language, as if he himself did not take himself or the poem seriously enough to want to make it heard *now* by all those beings in the midst of whom he must spend his life."[2] And here is a moment from a Kelly poem where the poet speaks to "all those beings":

Clarified into present

standing now in the stare of the vulture Jesus
watching the wings spread    the animal body writhe
leading to an immediate world
is Vision to be compromised in the glitter of steel
arched back of wildcat    tin leaves of the gumtree?

Kelly has written poetry unlike this fragment from "The Exchanges II," and the lines are of course without context, but would any context change them very much? The poet who wants to be heard by "all those beings" and who censures academics for their cringing bondage to past tones and literary forms takes himself so dead seriously that he cannot, evidently, afford to indulge in any recognizable tone of voice, with the result that in this poem nobody is speaking to nobody.

Granted that with the examples of Milton, Blake, and Pound in mind we do not always demand various tones of voice in a poem; by the nature of his task the prophetic poet must reach beyond the limits of his daily tonal self. Far and away the contemporary poet most successful at transcending considerations of tone is Allen Ginsberg, as in this scrap from "Poem Rocket" complete with picture of a rocket of sorts and an epigraph from Gregory Corso exhorting us winningly to "Be a Star-Screwer!":

[2] *A Controversy of Poets,* ed. Paris Leary and Robert Kelly (New York, 1965). Quotations of lines from poems by Kelly and Allen Ginsberg are taken from this anthology.

Old moon my eyes are new moon with human footprint
no longer Romeo Sadface in drunken river Loony Pierre
   eyebrow, goof moon
O possible moon in Heaven we get to first of ageless constellations of names
as God is possible as All is possible so we'll reach another
   life
Moon politicians earth weeping and warring in eternity
tho not one star disturbed by screaming madmen from
   Hollywood . . .

That the moon becomes "Romeo Sadface," that there are stars
in Hollywood too, are pieces of wit existing independently of
any tone of voice, certainly of "spoken American" (Davie's
phrase) played off against stanza-breaks or line-divisions. Ginsberg's Loony Pierre transformations and assertions of truth
are much more attractive, amusing, and acute than Robert
Kelly's solemn brand—which is to say that there are prophets
and prophets. But both poets are committed to not less than
star-screwing aspirations (". . . a radical breakthrough in the
nature of human consciousness and the nature of human verbal
understanding," in the words of Kelly's postscript), in the interests of which they short-circuit Frostian tensions between
rhythm and meter or wildness and fulfilled subject, and move
instead toward Pure Assertion.

Let us remind ourselves of the kind of poem Kelly and
Ginsberg and the nonacademic versifiers were fed up with and
resolved never to write. In this accomplished example by
Howard Moss the speaker, rather than addressing "all those
beings," decides to become a pruned tree:

   The Pruned Tree

   As a torn paper might seal up its side
   Or a streak of water stitch itself to silk

And disappear, my wound has been my healing,
And I am made more beautiful by losses.
See the flat water in the distance nodding
Approval, the light that fell in love with statues,
Seeing me alive, turn its motion toward me.
Shorn, I rejoice in what was taken from me.

What can the moonlight do with my new shape
But trace and retrace its miracle of order?
I stand, waiting for the strange reaction
Of insects who knew me in my larger self,
Unkempt, in a naturalness I did not love,
Even the dog's voice rings with a new echo,
And all the little leaves I shed are singing,
Singing to the moon of shapely newness.

Somewhere what I lost I hope is springing
To life again. The roofs, astonished by me,
Are taking new bearings in the night, the owl
Is crying for a further wisdom, the lilac
Putting forth its strongest scent to find me.
Butterflies, the sailboat's grooves, are winging
Out of the water to wash me, wash me.
Now, I am stirring like a seed in China.

No star-screwer he! We notice the reverent care with which
"s" and "w" sounds are varied; we experience the soft repeated caress of "singing,/ Singing" and "wash me, wash me."
But it is mention of "China" that establishes the impeccably
academic ring of this poem. Richard Eberhart in "The
Groundhog" (an earlier academic poem) "thought of China
and of Greece;" now with the aid of Kingsley Amis and
Philip Larkin we can resist such poetic thoughts, asking irrev-
erently whether the poet means *Red* China? Can there be any
wildness in a tune so timidly draped over the lines ("See the
flat water in the distance nodding/ Approval . . .") and sung

in a voice so enraptured with its own precious "miracle of order?" We may cry out with Robert Kelly: what good does it do me, do anybody, to hear this? Or with Ezra Pound: if poetry is news that stays news, what news has "The Pruned Tree" to give? Yet one thing the poem shares with Kelly's fragment is a solemn voice that drones on, whether about "tin leaves of the gumtree" or "Butterflies winging out of the water to wash me, wash me." The academic poem can have just as few dramatic tones of meaning struck across a meter, can be just as little a Frostian wild tune, as its revolutionary opposite.

If the existence of a wild poem rebukes that of a tame one, where do we look to find the wild lines that, extending Emerson's phrase, save the whole book of contemporary American poetry? The literary culture speaks rightly when it answers that we look to the poetry of Robert Lowell; but I want to suggest also the names of James Merrill, of Richard Wilbur, and above all of Randall Jarrell. These quite distinguishable poetic personalities share a large curiosity about things of this world, of legend, of the past, and of other poems. And perhaps because they are all extremely intelligent, learned, and witty poets, they act as if they took seriously Frost's cry at the end of his preface to Edwin Arlington Robinson's *King Jasper*:

> Give us immedicable woes—woes that nothing can be done for—woes flat and final. And then to play. The play's the thing. Play's the thing. All virtue in "as if."

How well Jarrell understood that advice, which Frost's prose practices as it preaches, can be seen in his superb essays about Frost but also in his own poems that over the course of Jarrell's career grew more woeful as they grew more playful.

Moving from Cheer to Joy, from Joy to All
I take a box
And add it to my wild rice, my Cornish game hens.
The slacked or shorted, basketed, identical
Food-gathering flocks
Are selves I overlook. Wisdom, said William James

Is learning what to overlook. And I am wise
If that is wisdom.
Yet somehow, as I buy All from these shelves
And the boy takes it to my station wagon,
What I've become
Troubles me even if I shut my eyes. . . .

These stanzas are only the beginning of the late monologue "Next Day," in which a middle-aged woman confronts her life, but they are enough to establish how the play springs from woe, from griefs rather than grievances, as Frost puts it elsewhere in the Robinson preface. Jarrell's woman is of course no ordinary lady in a supermarket, equipped as she is with a memory of William James, and extraordinarily adept at moving within the poetic line from one detergent to another; so we are not surprised when the word "overlook" takes on even further resonance as the grocery boy neglects to look at her and she is bewildered that it should be so. The voice which speaks the poem is both within and outside her experience: the play's the thing.

Play is also the thing when the poet speaks for himself in "Aging":

I wake, but before I know it it is done,
The day, I sleep. And of days like these the years,
A life is made. I nod, consenting to my life.
. . . But who can live in these quick-passing hours?

I need to find again, to make a life,
A child's Sunday afternoon, the Pleasure Drive
Where everything went by but time; the Study Hour
Spent at a desk, with folded hands, in waiting.

In those I could make. Did I not make in them
Myself? The Grown One whose time shortens,
Breath quickens, heart beats faster, till at last
It catches, skips. . . . Yet those hours that seemed, were
     endless
Were still not long enough to have remade
My childish heart: the heart that must have, always,
To make anything of anything, not time,
Not time but—
          but, alas! eternity.

There is much to stumble over in the less than flawless rhythm
of this lament, while the voice works within a fairly quiet
range of feeling. Yet within that range how much variety of
nuance occurs as we follow the changes rung on the verb
"make" or observe the relaxed superiority of memory that recalls in capital letters a child's Pleasure Drive or the Study
Hour, then comes up sharply and painfully against another
fixity—the Grown One, finished and yet not even begun. The
poem has its burden of woes flat and final that nothing can be
done for; yet looked at again the whole affair is a kind of
joke (imagine needing more than *time* to remake yourself!)
which when understood makes life no less woeful, but gives
us another way to feel about the woe. Even the silence of the
second ellipsis seems bristling with an expressed tone of regard,
as if one can only throw up his hands in the face of such a
living joke. For as long as the poem lasts we believe that nothing in nor out of the world could reduce its voice to a monotone.

Whether one agrees with the claims of value I make for Jarrell's voice, there can be no denying that something quite different has been developing in several highly regarded poets of the sixties whose main work seems to be a rejection of what Frost, Jarrell, and Lowell represent and embody. I refer here not to the Black Mountain group, the loosely associated Olson-Duncan-Creeley triumvirate with which Robert Kelly has affiliations, and whose principles and interests run no risk of being confused with Frost's, but to an even more loosely associated one—a group only in that its members often write poems which resemble each other's. These poems feature an "I" released from most of the ordinary all-too-human desires encountered, for example, in Jarrell's poems; an "I" that is above, or at the point of transcending, the agonies and strifes of human hearts. Annunciations by the would-be transcender are made in a relatively toneless mode; they are usually portentous, more often than not humorless, and they seldom make use of the syntactical windings, the risings and fallings of spoken American over the line that, again, are so important in Jarrell's work. Here are three brief excerpts from some on-the-road poems by poets of what might be termed the somnambulistic school:

I dream of journeys continually:
Of flying like a bat deep into a narrowing tunnel,
Of driving alone, without luggage, out a long peninsula,
The road lined with snow-laden second growth
A fine dry snow ticking the windshield
Alternate snow and sleet, no on-coming traffic,
And no lights behind, in the blurred side-mirror
The road changing from glazed tarface to a rubble of
    stone . . .

(Theodore Roethke, "The Far Field")

Just off the highway to Rochester, Minnesota,
Twilight bounds softly forth on the grass
And the eyes of those two Indian ponies
Darken with kindness.
They have come gladly out of the willows
To welcome my friend and me. . . .
        Suddenly I realize
That if I stepped out of my body I would break
Into blossom.
                        (James Wright, "A Blessing")


I look out at the white sleet covering the still streets
As we drive through Scarsdale—
The sleet began falling as we left Connecticut,
And the wet winter leaves swirled in the wet air after cars
Like hands suddenly turned over in a conversation.
Now the frost has nearly buried the short green grass of
        March
Seeing the sheets of sleet untouched on the wide streets
I think of the many comfortable homes stretching for
        miles . . .
                (Robert Bly, "Sleet Storm on the Merritt Parkway")


Further candidates for this school might be James Dickey, W.
S. Merwin, Donald Justice, Mark Strand: in the interests of
directness, of sincerity in depth, they eschew an ironic social
tone and choose a purer toneless voice which would somehow
encompass Life itself. Though this account simplifies the varieties of poetry in Roethke and in Dickey, in particular, I believe it points to a central quality of sensibility in each. But
taken as a group, if play is the thing there seems to be little
play in the poems of these writers between moments of identifiable tone and other moments which stand out strongly by

their comparative lack of tone. It is the paradox of their purity that the move beyond play toward Life gives at least one reader a push in the opposite direction.

Death is what Robert Lowell's poetry saves us from, in Frost's sense of salvation through the figure of a poem that ends with a clarification of life—"not a great clarification, such as sects and cults are founded on, but in a momentary stay against confusion." What better title for the key volume of this poetry than *Life Studies?* And if, as Donald Davie has it in the essay referred to earlier, American poets deal in agony while their British counterparts settle for discomfort, it would seem that the final and most famous poem in the volume is about such agony, about woes flat and final. Only the *way* it is about them makes all the difference:

Skunk Hour
(*For Elizabeth Bishop*)

Nautilus Island's hermit
heiress still lives through winter in her Spartan cottage
her sheep still graze above the sea.
Her son's a bishop. Her farmer
is first selectman in our village;
she's in her dotage.

Thirsting for
the hierarchic privacy
of Queen Victoria's century,
she buys up all
the eyesores facing her shore,
and lets them fall.

The season's ill—
we've lost our summer millionaire,

who seemed to leap from an L. L. Bean
catalogue. His nine-knot yawl
was auctioned off to lobstermen.
A red fox stain covers Blue Hill.

And now our fairy
decorator brightens his shop for fall;
his fishnet's filled with orange cork,
orange, his cobbler's bench and awl;
there is no money in his work,
he'd rather marry.

One dark night,
my Tudor Ford climbed the hill's skull;
I watched for love-cars. Lights turned down,
they lay together, hull to hull
where the graveyard shelves on the town. . . .
My mind's not right.

A car radio bleats
"Love, O careless Love. . . ." I hear
my ill-spirit sob in each blood cell,
as if my hand were at its throat. . . .
I myself am hell;
nobody's here—

only skunks, that search
in the moonlight for a bite to eat.
They march on their soles up Main Street:
white stripes, moonstruck eyes' red fire
under the chalk-dry and spar spire
of the Trinitarian Church.

I stand on top
of our back steps and breathe the rich air—
a mother skunk with her column of kittens swills the garbage
        pail.

She jabs her wedge-head in a cup
of sour cream, drops her ostrich tail,
and will not scare.

Seekers after sensation may pick out phrases like "My mind's not right," excite themselves with talk about mental institutions and gossip about Lowell's biography, and fancy they are in the presence of raw meat, pure wildness at last. More dutiful but more to be pitied students may pick up one of those casebook interpretations of Lowell's poetry and duly encounter the following at the end of a long analysis of "Skunk Hour":

> In an ironic and muted way the skunk becomes . . . a symbol of hope for the speaker, an example to him in her brave indifference. The speaker, moreover, is also brave, and his effort to confront the Self carries with it by implication the redeeming character of self-recognition and the therapeutic value of personal confession. Man can live with his hell, or gain strength by feeding on the garbage of our civilization, the poem seems to say, so long as he can articulate his experience, and furthermore, contained within the hell is the clear reality of something better, to breathe the rich air, or to be a healthy skunk.[3]

This lamentable tale told by the critic as he plasters Meaning all over the poem is told on too many sides, in too many casebooks and essays, with too much interpretative enthusiasm or self-righteousness. It tames the wildness of "Skunk Hour" by refusing to submit to its tune, by translating its images and utterances into sociological categories of understanding, by regarding tone of voice with iron inattention.

[3] William J. Martz, *The Achievement of Robert Lowell* (Glenview, Ill., 1966), p. 12.

What is an alternative way to behaving as if the poem were thrilling gossip or a timely commentary on our civilization? Instead of translating "My mind's not right" into what it "means"—I am a perverted voyeur—suppose we located the "I" within the figure the poem makes: his mind's not right, but what about Nautilus Island's hermit heiress in her dotage? Suppose *your* son was a bishop—how would *you* feel? And what about the mind of the summer millionaire gone God knows where after his brilliant leap from the L. L. Bean catalogue? Or, most splendid and saddest of all, the Fairy Decorator who, after a brief moment of poetic glory so rich and strange that only quasi-chiastic word order will suffice to express it—"his fishnet's filled with orange cork,/ orange, his cobbler's bench and awl"—is brought down to earth, an ill-spirit too, so disenchanted he'd rather marry.

In an odd and interesting sense the "I" of "Skunk Hour" must compete with heiresses, millionaires, and fairy decorators —all creations of the poet; thus a voice which in one stanza immortalizes the decorator, then in the next makes claims for his own mind not being right, is something more than a lyric cry for help. Help has already been provided; the striking histrionics of "I myself am hell;/ nobody's here" are set off, tempered, and made more humanly inclusive by the logic of other observations, characters, and events. A funny kind of logic to be sure that gives shape and amusing comprehension to millionaires and fairy decorators as well as to the marvelous beings which title the poem:

> I myself am hell;
> nobody's here—
>
> only skunks, that search
> in the moonlight for a bite to eat.

They march on their soles up Main Street:
white stripes, moonstruck eyes' red fire
under the chalk-dry and spar spire
of the Trinitarian Church.

The skunks veritably push aside the speaker's ill-spirit: as they
march along, the stresses grow heavier and the rhyming becomes broad and loud (earlier in the casual introduction of
village characters it had been designedly "off"), and not only
at line ends but within them as well. Note the catchy insouci-
ance of "in the moonlight for a bite to eat," a jaunty tune from
the thirties perhaps. Lowell has said that this poem has no
meter within the line, yet the Frostian play of a speaking voice
against at least the ghost of meter is very much felt. And play
it is too:

She jabs her wedge-head in a cup
of sour cream, drops her ostrich tail,
and will not scare.

To run over a line and come upon sour cream at the beginning
of the next one indicates a poetic air at least as rich as that
breathed on the back steps in Maine. What do the skunks stand
for, mean, represent, symbolize? Nature, the World, Good,
Evil, Good-and-Evil, Hope, Despair? One fills in the blanks, as
did the interpreter quoted earlier, only at one's peril; for in the
truly playful poem the blanks are already filled in—with
skunks. And the "I" has been located with serious comedy,
placed by the figure of a poem in which wildness and logic
combine more intimately than they do in Blue Hill, Maine, or
other places known to man.

Robert Lowell's achievement has been praised for "reaffirming the power of literature to order the chaos of society, personality and history, with its own history, its own order, its own virtue," and for reassuring us of "the survival of literature itself." At a time when even the universities are full of passionate intensity and the drive is toward sincere, open-ended, unstructured communication—either outside or inside poems—it may be refreshing to turn to the other poems of our climate, that climate I have been partially charting with the phrase Wildness of Logic. Here the utterance is deep and playful, made from gestures of revelation *and* of reticence, of straight talk and obliquity: the lyric impulse to soar in contention and cooperation with a wryly satiric and earthbound one; dream and fact engaging in their endless argument. And the poetry which gives expression to these impulses invites us not to interpret it so much as to respond with a criticism half as flexible, as playful as its object. Wallace Stevens has described it as

> a violence from within that protects us from a violence without. It is the imagination pressing back against the pressure of reality. It seems in the last analysis, to have something to do with our self-preservation; and that, no doubt, is why the expression of it, the sound of its words, helps us to live our lives.[4]

No tears in the writer, no tears in the reader, says Frost. To which we might add, no play in the reader, no play in the poem: the poet helps those readers who help themselves.

[4] Wallace Stevens, *The Necessary Angel* (New York, 1965), p. 36.

PAUL DE MAN

# Lyric and Modernity

MY title and procedure call for some preliminary clarification before I get involved in the technicalities of detailed exegesis. I am not concerned, in this paper, with a descriptive characterization of contemporary poetry but with the problem of literary modernity in general. The term "modernity" is not used in a simple chronological sense as an approximate synonym for "recent" or "contemporary" with a positive or negative value-emphasis added. It designates more generally the problematical possibility of all literature to exist in the present, to be considered, or read, from a point of view that claims to share with it its own sense of a temporal present. In theory, the question of modernity could therefore be asked of any literature at any time, contemporaneous or not. In practice, however, the question has to be put somewhat more pragmatically from a point of view that postulates a roughly contemporaneous perspective and that favors recent over older literature. This necessity is inherent in the ambivalent status of the term "modernity," which is itself partly pragmatic and descriptive, partly conceptual and normative. In the common usage of the word the pragmatic implications usually over-shadow theoretical possibilities that remain unexplored. My emphasis tries to restore this balance to some degree: hence the stress on literary categories and dimensions that exist inde-pendently of historical contingencies, the main concession be-ing that the examples are chosen from so-called modern literature and criticism. The conclusions however, could, with some minor modifications, be transferred to other historical periods and be applicable whenever or wherever literature as such occurs.

What is thus assumed to be possible in time—and it is a mere assumption, since the compromise or theorizing about examples chosen on pragmatic grounds in fact begs the question and postpones the issue—can much more easily be justified in geo-graphical, spatial terms. My examples are taken primarily from French and German literature and the polemical aspects of the argument are directed against a trend prevalent among a rela-tively small group of German scholars, a group that is repre-sentative but by no means predominant in continental criticism. But it should not be difficult to find equivalent texts and criti-cal attitudes in English or American literature; the indirect route by way of France and Germany should allow for a clearer view of the local scene, once the necessary transitions have been made. The natural expansion of the paper would lie in this direction.

With modernity thus conceived as a general and theoretical rather than as a historical theme, it is not a priori certain that it should be treated differently with regard to lyric poetry as opposed to, for example, narrative prose or the drama. Can the factual distinction between prose, poetry, and the drama rele-vantly be extended to modernity, a notion that is not inher-

ently bound to any particular genre? Can we find out something about the nature of modernity by relating it to lyric
poetry that we could not find out in dealing with novels or
plays? Here again, the point of departure has to be chosen for
reasons of expediency rather than for theoretical reasons, in the
hope that the expediency may eventually receive theoretical
confirmation. It is an established fact that, in contemporary
criticism, the question of modernity is asked in a somewhat
different manner with regard to lyric poetry than with regard
to prose. Genre concepts seem somehow to be sensitive to the
idea of modernity, thus suggesting a possible differentiation
between them in terms of their temporal structures—since
modernity is, in essence, a temporal notion. Yet the link between modernity and the basic genres is far from clear. On the
one hand, lyric poetry is often seen not as an evolved but as an
early and spontaneous form of language, in open contrast to
more self-conscious and reflective, prosaic forms of literary
discourse. In eighteenth-century speculations about the origins
of language, it is a commonplace to assert that the archaic language is that of poetry, the contemporary or modern language
that of prose. Vico, Rousseau, and Herder, to mention only the
most famous names, all assert the priority of poetry over prose,
often with a value-emphasis that seems to interpret the loss of
spontaneity as a decline—although this particular aspect of
eighteenth-century primitivism is in fact a great deal less single-
minded and uniform in the authors themselves than in their
later interpreters. Be this as it may, it remains that, regardless
of value judgments, the definition of poetry as the first language gives it an archaic, ancient quality that is the opposite of
modern, whereas the deliberate, cold, and rational character of
discursive prose, which can only imitate or represent the original impulse if it does not ignore it altogether, would be the
true language of modernity. The same assumption appears al-

ready during the eighteenth century, with "music" substituting
for "poetry" and opposed to language or literature as an
equivalent of prose. This becomes, as is well known, a commonplace of post-symbolist aesthetics, still present in writers
such as Valéry or Proust, though here perhaps in an ironic
context that has not always been recognized as such. Music is
seen, as Proust puts it, as a unified, preanalytical "communication of the soul," a "possibility that remained without sequel
[because] mankind chose other ways, those of spoken and
written language."[1] In this nostalgic primitivism—which Proust
is "demystifying" rather than sharing—the music of poetry and
the rationality of prose are opposed as ancient is opposed to
modern. Within this perspective, it would be an absurdity to
speak of the modernity of lyric poetry, since the lyric is precisely the antithesis of modernity.

Yet, in our own twentieth century, the social projection of
modernity known as the avant-garde consisted predominantly
of poets rather than of prose writers. The most aggressively
modern literary movements of the century, surrealism and ex-
pressionism, in no way value prose over poetry, the dramatic
or the narrative over the lyric. In the recent past, this trend
may have changed. One speaks readily, in contemporary
French literature, of a *nouveau roman*, but not of a *nouvelle
poésie*. French structuralist "new criticism" is much more concerned with narrative prose than with poetry and sometimes
rationalizes this preference into an overtly antipoetic aesthetics.
But this is in part a local phenomenon, a reaction against a traditional bias in French criticism in favor of poetry, perhaps
also an innocent rejoicing like that of a child that has been

---

[1] Marcel Proust, *A la recherche du temps perdu*, ed. Pierre Clarac
and André Ferré, Pléiade edition (Paris, 1954), Vol. III, "La Prison-
nière," p. 258.

given a new toy. The discovery that there are critical devices suitable for the analysis of prose is by no means such a sensational novelty for English and American critics, in whom these new French studies of narrative modes may awaken a more sedate feeling of *déjà vu*. In Germany, however, among critics that are by no means adverse or ideologically opposed to the contemporary French schools, lyric poetry remains the preferred topic of investigation for a definition of modernity. The editors of a recent symposium on the subject "The Lyric as Paradigm of Modernity" assert as a matter of course that "the lyric was chosen as paradigmatic for the evolution toward modern literature, because the breakdown of literary forms occurred earlier and can be better documented in this genre than in any other."[2] Here then, far from being judged absurd, the question of modernity in the lyric is considered as the best means of access to a discussion of literary modernity in general. In purely historical terms, this position is certainly sensible: it would be impossible to speak relevantly about modern literature without giving a prominent place to lyric poetry: some of the most suggestive theoretical writing on modernity is to be found in essays dealing with poetry. Nevertheless, the tension that develops between poetry and prose when they are considered within the perspective of modernity is far from meaningless; the question is complex enough to have to be postponed until well beyond the point we can hope to reach in this paper.

When Yeats, in 1936, had to write the introduction to his anthology of modern English poetry, he mainly used the op-

[2] *Immanente Ästhetik, Ästhetische Reflexion: Lyrik als Paradigma der Moderne,* ed. W. Iser, Poetik und Hermeneutik, Arbeitsergebnisse einer Forschungsgruppe II (Munich, 1966), p. 4.

portunity, in a text that otherwise shows more traces of fatigue
than of inspiration, to set himself apart from Eliot and Pound
as more modern than they, using Walter James Turner and
Dorothy Wellesley as props to represent a truly modern tendency of which he considered himself to be the main representative. That he also had the courage of his convictions is made
clear by the fact that he allotted to himself, in the body of the
anthology, twice as much space as to anyone else—with the
sole exception of Oliver St. John Gogarty, hardly a dangerous
rival. The theoretical justification given for this claim is slight
but, in the light of later developments, quite astute. The opposition between "good" and modern poetry—his own—and not
so good and not so modern poetry—mainly Eliot's and Pound's
—is made in terms of a contrast between poetry of representation and a poetry that would no longer be mimetic. The
mimetic poetry has for its emblem the mirror, somewhat in-
congruously associated with Stendhal, though it is revealing
that the reference is to a writer of prose and that the prosaic
element in Eliot's precision and in Pound's chaos are under
attack. This is a poetry depending on an outside world, regardless of whether this world is seen in neat, objective contours or
as shapeless flux. Much less easy to characterize is the other
kind of poetry, said to be of the "private soul . . . always behind our knowledge, though always hidden . . . the sole source
of pain, stupefaction, evil."[3] Its emblem, as we all know from
Meyer Abrams if not necessarily from Yeats, is the lamp,
though here Abrams's stroke of genius in singling out this
emblematic pair for the title of his book on romantic literary
theory is perhaps slightly misleading, not in terms of the poetics of romanticism but with regard to Yeats's own meaning.

[3] *Oxford Book of Modern Verse, 1892–1935*, ed. W. B. Yeats
(New York, 1936), Introduction, p. XXXI.

In Abrams's book, the lamp becomes the symbol of the constitutive, autonomous self, the creative subjectivity that certainly looms large in romantic theory, as an analogous microcosm of the world of nature. The light of that lamp is the self-knowledge of a consciousness, an internalized metaphor of daylight vision; mirror and lamp are both symbols of light, whatever their further differences and oppositions may be. But Yeats's lamp is not that of the self, but of what he calls the "soul," and self and soul, as we know from his poetry, are antithetical. Soul does not, at any rate, belong to the realm of natural or artificial (i.e., represented or imitated) light, but to that of sleep and darkness. It does not dwell in real or copied nature, but rather in the kind of wisdom that lies hidden away in books. To the extent that it is private and inward, the soul resembles the self, and only by ways of the self (and not by ways of nature) can one find access to it. But one has to move through the self beyond the self, and truly modern poetry is a poetry that has become aware of the incessant conflict that opposes a self, still engaged in the daylight world of reality, of representation, and of life, to what Yeats calls the soul. Translated into terms of poetic diction, this implies that modern poetry uses an imagery that is both symbol and allegory, that represents objects in nature but is actually taken from purely literary sources. The tension between these two modes of language also puts in question the autonomy of the self. Modern poetry is described by Yeats as the conscious expression of a conflict within the function of language as representation and within the conception of language as the act of an autonomous self.

Some literary historians, who necessarily approached the problem of modern poetry in a less personal way, have written about modern lyric poetry in strikingly similar terms. Hugo Friedrich, one of the last representatives of a group of outstanding Romanic scholars of German origin that includes Vossler, Curtius, Auerbach, and Leo Spitzer, has exercised a great deal of influence through his short book *The Structure of the Modern Lyric*.[4] Friedrich uses the traditional historical pattern, also present in Marcel Raymond's *From Baudelaire to Surrealism*, making French poetry of the nineteenth century and especially Baudelaire the starting point of a movement that spread to the whole body of Western lyric poetry. His main concern, understandably enough in an explicator of texts, is the particular difficulty and obscurity of modern poetry, an obscurity not unrelated to the light-symbolism of Yeats's mirror and lamp. The cause of the specifically modern kind of obscurity—which Friedrich to some extent deplores—resides for him, as for Yeats, in a loss of the representational function of poetry that goes parallel with the loss of a sense of selfhood. Loss of representational reality (*Entrealisierung*) and loss of self (*Entpersönlichung*) go hand in hand: "With Baudelaire, the depersonalization of the modern lyric starts, at least in the sense that the lyrical voice is no longer the expression of a unity between the work and the empirical person, a unity that the romantics, contrary to several centuries of earlier lyrical poetry, had tried to achieve."[5] And in Baudelaire "idealization no longer, as in the older aesthetic, strives toward an embellishment of reality but strives for loss of reality." Modern poetry —this is said with reference to Rimbaud—"is no longer concerned with a reader. It does not want to be understood. It is a hallucinatory storm, flashes of lightning hoping at most to

[4] Hugo Friedrich, *Die Struktur der Modernen Lyrik*, expanded edition (Hamburg, 1967). By May, 1967, 111,000 copies of this book had been printed.

[5] Quotations in this paragraph and the next are (in order) from *ibid.*, pp. 36, 56, 84, 53, and 44. All translations and italics are my own.

create the fear before danger that stems from an attraction toward danger. They are texts without self, without 'I.' For the self that appears from time to time is the artificial, alien self projected in the *lettre du voyant.*" Ultimately, the function of representation is entirely taken over by sound effects without reference to any meaning whatever.

Friedrich offers no theoretical reasons why the loss of representation—it would be more accurate to speak of a putting into question or an ambivalence of representation—and the loss of self—with the same qualification—are thus linked. He gives instead the crudest extraneous and pseudo-historical explanation of this tendency as a mere escape from a reality that is said to have become gradually more unpleasant ever since the middle of the nineteenth century. Gratuitous fantasies, ". . . the absurd," he writes, "become aspects of irreality into which Baudelaire and his followers want to penetrate, *in order to* avoid an increasingly confining reality." Critical overtones of morbidity and decadence are unmistakable, and the possibility of reading Friedrich's book as an indictment of modern poetry—a thesis nowhere explicitly stated by the author—is certainly not entirely foreign to the considerable popular success of the book. Here again, it is preferable for the sake of clarity to put the value judgment temporarily between brackets. Friedrich's historicist background, however crude, and his suggestion that the evolution of modern literature follows a line that is part of a wider historical pattern allow him to give his essay a genetic historical coherence. A continuous genetic chain links the work of Baudelaire to that of his successors Mallarmé, Rimbaud, Valéry, and their counterparts in the other European literatures. The chain extends in both directions, for Friedrich finds antecedents of the modern trend as far back as Rousseau and Diderot, and makes romanticism a link in the same chain. Symbolist and post-symbolist poetry appear therefore as a later, more self-conscious but also more morbid version of certain romantic insights; both form a historical continuum in which distinctions can be made only in terms of degree, not of kind, or in terms of extrinsic considerations, ethical, psychological, sociological, or purely formal. A similar view is represented in this country by Meyer Abrams, for example, in a paper entitled "Coleridge, Baudelaire and Modernist Poetics" published in 1964.

This scheme is so satisfying to our inherent sense of historical order that it has rarely been challenged, even by some who would not in the least agree with its potential ideological implications. Thus we find a group of younger German scholars, whose evaluation of modernity would be strongly opposed to what is implied by Friedrich, still adhering to exactly the same historical scheme. Hans Robert Jauss and some of his colleagues have considerably refined the diagnosis of obscurity that Friedrich had made the center of his analysis. Their understanding of medieval and baroque literature—which Friedrich chose to use in a merely contrastive way when writing on the modern lyric—influenced by fundamental reinterpretations of the kind that made it possible for a critic such as Walter Benjamin to speak about sixteenth-century literature and about Baudelaire in closely similar terms, allows them to describe Friedrich's *Entrealisierung* and *Entpersönlichung* with a new stylistic rigor. The traditional term of allegory that Benjamin, perhaps more than anyone else in Germany, helped to restore in some of its full implications is frequently used by them to describe a tension within the language that can no longer be modeled on the subject-object relationships derived from experiences of perception, or from theories of the imagination derived from perception. In an earlier essay, Benjamin had suggested that "the intensity of the interrelationship between the perceptual and the intellectual element"[6] be made the main concern of the interpreter of poetry. This indicates that the assumed correspondence between meaning and object is put into question. From this point on, the very presence of any outward object can become superfluous, and, in an important article published in 1960, H. R. Jauss characterizes an allegorical style as "beauté inutile," the absence of any reference to an exterior reality of which it would be the sign. The "disappearance of the object" has become the main theme.[7] This development is seen as a historical process that can be more or less accurately dated: in the field of lyric poetry, Baudelaire is still named as the originator of a modern allegorical style. Friedrich's historical pattern survives, though now based on linguistic and rhetorical rather than on superficially sociological considerations. A student of Jauss, Karlheinz Stierle, tries to document this scheme in a consecutive reading of three poems by Nerval, Mallarmé, and Rimbaud, showing the gradual process of irrealization dialectically at work in these three texts.[8]

[6] ". . . die Intensität der Verbundenheit der anschaulichen und der geistigen Elemente." Walter Benjamin, "Zwei Gedichte von Hölderlin," in *Schriften*, II (Frankfurt a. M., 1955), 377.

[7] Hans Robert Jauss, "Zur Frage der Struktureinheit älterer und moderner Lyrik," *GRM*, XLI (1960), 266.

[8] Karlheinz Stierle, "Möglichkeiten des dunklen Stils in den Anfängen moderner Lyrik in Frankreich," in *Lyrik als Paradigma der Moderne*, pp. 157–94. My argument is more polemical in tone than in substance. Some of the doubts expressed about the possibility of a nonrepresentational poetry are conceded by K. Stierle himself in a later addition to his original paper (*ibid.*, pp. 193–94). The possibility of complete "irrealization" asserted in the analysis of the Mallarmé text is thus put into question. Rather than by the contrast between literature and painting suggested by Stierle, I approach the problem in terms of a contrast between a genetic concept of literary history and modernity.

Stierle's detailed reading of a late and difficult sonnet by
Mallarmé can serve as a model for the discussion of the *idées
reçues* that this group of scholars still shares with Friedrich, all
political appearances to the contrary. His interpretation of the
*Tombeau de Verlaine*—chronologically though not stylistically
perhaps Mallarmé's last text—following Benjamin's dictum,
consciously analyzes the obscurity of the poem, the resistance
of the diction to a definitive meaning or set of meanings, as the
interpenetration between intellectual and perceptual elements.
And Stierle comes to the conclusion that, at least in certain
lines of the poem, the sensory elements have entirely vanished.
At the beginning of the sonnet, an actual object—a tombstone
—is introduced:

> Le noir roc courroucé que la bise le roule

but this actual object, according to Stierle, is "at once transcended into irreality by a movement that cannot be represented." As for the second stanza, "it can no longer be referred
to an exterior reality." Although Mallarmé's poetry, more than
any other (including Baudelaire's or Nerval's), uses objects
rather than subjective feelings or inward emotions, this apparent return to objects (*Vergegenständlichung*), far from aug-
menting our sense of reality, of language adequately represent-
ing the object, is in fact a subtle and successful strategy to
achieve complete irreality. For the logic of the relationships
that exist between the various objects in the poem is no longer
based on the logic of nature or of representation, but on a
purely intellectual and allegorical logic decreed and maintained
by the poet in total defiance of natural events. "The situation
of the poem," writes Stierle, referring to the dramatic action
that takes place between the various "things" that appear in it,

"can no longer be represented in sensory terms. . . . If we con-
sider, not the object but that which makes it unreal, then this
is a poetry of allegorical reification (*Vergegenständlichung*).
One is struck most of all by the nonrepresentability of what is
assumedly being shown: the stone rolling by its own will. . . .
In traditional allegory, the function of the concrete image was to
make the meaning stand out more vividly. The *sensus allegori-
cus*, as a concrete representation, acquired a new clarity. But
for Mallarmé the concrete image no longer leads to a clearer
vision. The unity reached on the level of the object can no
longer be represented. And it is precisely this unreal constellation that is intended as the product of the poetic activity." This
particular Mallarmean strategy is seen as a development leading
beyond Baudelaire, whose allegory is still centered on a subject
and psychologically motivated. Mallarmé's modernity stems
from the impersonality of an allegorical (i.e., nonrepresentational) diction entirely freed from a subject. The historical
continuity from Baudelaire to Mallarmé follows a genetic
movement of gradual allegorization and depersonalization.

The test of such a theory has to be found in the quality of
the exegetic work performed by its proponent. Returning to
the text, we can confine ourselves to one or two of the key
words that play an important part in Stierle's argument. First
of all, the word "roc" in the first line:

Le noir roc courroucé que la bise le roule

The movement of this rock, driven by the cold north wind, is
said by Stierle to be "at once" beyond representation. As we
know from the actual occasion for which the poem was written
and which is alluded to in the title, as well as from the other
*Tombeaux* poems of Mallarmé on Poe, Gautier, and Baudelaire,

this rock indeed represents the monument of Verlaine's grave around which a group of writers gathered to celebrate the first anniversary of his death. The thought that such a stone could be made to move by the sheer force of the wind, and that it could then be halted (or tried to be halted) by applying hands to it ("Ne s'arrêtera ni sous de pieuses mains/ Tâtant sa ressemblance avec les maux humains"), is indeed absurd from a representational point of view. Equally absurd is the pseudo-representational phrase that combines a literal action ("tâter") with an abstraction ("la ressemblance"), made more unreal yet because the resemblance is in its turn to something general and abstract ("la ressemblance avec les maux humains"). We are supposed to touch not a stone but the resemblance of a stone, wandering about driven by the wind, to a human emotion. Stierle certainly seems to have a point when he characterizes this dramatic "situation" as beyond representation.

But why should the significance of "roc" be restricted to one single meaning? At the furthest remove from the literal reading, we can think of the rock in purely emblematic terms as the stone miraculously removed from the grave of a sacrificial figure and allowing for the metamorphosis of Christ from an earthly into a heavenly body; such a miracle could easily be accomplished by an allegorical, divine wind. There is nothing farfetched in such a reference. The circumstance of the poem is precisely the "empty tomb" (to quote Yeats) that honors the spiritual entity of Verlaine's work and not his bodily remains. Verlaine himself, in *Sagesse*, singled out by Mallarmé as his most important work,[9] constantly sees his own destiny as an *Imitatio Christi* and, at his death, much was made of the redeeming virtue of suffering for the repenting sinner. In

[9] Mallarmé, *Oeuvres complètes*, ed. Henri Modor and G. Jean-Aubry, Pléiade edition (Paris, 1945), p. 873.

Mallarmé's short prose texts on Verlaine, one senses his irritation with a facile Christianization of the poet, left to die in poverty and scorned as the alcoholic tramp that he was during his lifetime, but whose destiny becomes overnight a lesson in Christian redemption. This sentimental rehabilitation of Verlaine as a Christ figure, alluded to in the reference to the miracle of the Ascension, making his death exemplary for the suffering of all mankind, goes directly against Mallarmé's own conception of poetic immortality. The real movement of the work, its future destiny and correct understanding, will not be halted ("ne s'arrêtera pas") by such hypocritical piety. The opposition against a conventional Christian notion of death as redemption, a theme that recurs constantly in all the *Tombeaux* poems with their undeniable Masonic overtones, is introduced from the start by an emblematic reading of "roc" as an allusion to Scripture.[10]

What concerns us most for our argument is that the word "roc" thus can have several meanings and that, within the system of meanings thus set up, a different representational logic can be expected to function; within the scriptural context of miraculous events we can no longer expect naturalistic consistency. But between the literal rock of the gravestone and the emblematic rock of Christ's tomb, many intermediary readings are possible. In another prose text of Mallarmé's on Verlaine (that Stierle never mentions) Verlaine, later called tramp (vagabond) in the poem, is seen as a victim of the cold,

[10] The same polemical tone is apparent in a brief prose text written for the same occasion, the first anniversary of Verlaine's death (January 15, 1897) (Pléiade edition, p. 865). The sonnet, which appeared in *La Revue blanche* of January 1, 1897, actually precedes this text.

of solitude, and of poverty.[11] On another level, "roc" can then
designate Verlaine himself, whose dark and hulking shape can
without too much visual effort be seen as a "noir roc." And the
black object driven by a cold wind in the month of January
suggests still another meaning: that of a dark cloud. In Mallarmé's poems of this period (one thinks of *Un Coup de Dés*,
of "A la nue accablante tu," etc.) the cloud symbolism plays a
prominent part and would almost have to enter into the symbolic paraphernalia of any poem—since Mallarmé strives for
the inclusion of his entire symbolic apparatus in each text,
however brief it may be. The hidden cloud imagery in this
sonnet, first perceived by the intuitive but astute Mallarmé
reader Thibaudet in a commentary on the poem, which Stierle
mentions,[12] reappears in the second stanza and completes the
cosmic symbolic system that starts out "here" ("ici," in line 5),
on this pastoral earth, and ascends, by way of the cloud, to the
highest hierarchy of the star in line 7: ". . . l'astre mûri des
lendemains/ Dont un scintillement argentera les foules." With
a little ingenuity, more meanings could still be added, always

---

[11] "La solitude, le froid, l'inélégance et la pénurie d'ordinaire
composent le sort qu'encourt l'enfant . . . marchant en l'existence
selon sa divinité . . ." (Pléiade edition, p. 511). This text was written
at the time of Verlaine's death (January 9, 1896) and predates the
sonnet by one year. Gardner Davies (*Les Poèmes commémoratifs
de Mallarmé, essai d'exégèse raisonnée* [Paris, 1950], p. 191) quotes
the passage as a gloss on "maux humains" in line 3 but states, without further evidence, that the tombstone unambiguously represents
Verlaine (p. 189).

[12] Stierle, p. 174. The reference is to A. Thibaudet, *La Poésie de
Stéphane Mallarmé* (Paris, 1926), pp. 307–8. The same passage from
Thibaudet is quoted by Emilie Noulet, *Vingt poèmes de Stéphane
Mallarmé* (Paris, 1967), p. 259, whose commentary on this poem
generally follows Davies.

bearing in mind the auto-exegetic symbolic vocabulary that Mallarmé has developed by this time: thus the word "roule," written in 1897, suggests a cross-reference to the rolling of the dice in *Un Coup de Dés*, making the "roc" into a symbolical equivalent of the dice. And so on: the more relevant symbolic meanings one can discover, the closer one comes to the spirit of Mallarmé's metaphorical play in his later vocabulary.

"Noir roc" for a cloud may seem visually farfetched and forced, but it is not visually absurd. The process that takes us from the literal rock to Verlaine, to a cloud and the tomb of Christ, in an ascending curve from earth to heaven, has a certain representational, naturalistic consistency. We easily recognize it for the traditional poetic *topos* that it is, a metamorphosis, with exactly the degree of naturalistic verisimilitude that one would have to expect in this case. The entire poem is in fact a poem about a metamorphosis, the change brought about by death that transformed the actual person Verlaine in the intellectual abstraction of his work, "tel qu'en lui-même enfin l'éternité le change," with emphasis on the metamorphosis implied in "change." Confining himself to the single literal meaning of "roc," Stierle can rightly say that no representational element is at play in the text, but he also has to lose the main part of the meaning. A considerable extension of meaning, consistent with the thematic concerns of Mallarmé's other works of the same period, is brought about by allowing for the metamorphosis of one object into a number of other symbolic referents. Regardless of the final importance or value of Mallarmé's poetry as *statement*, the semantic plurality has to be taken into account at all stages, even and especially if the ultimate "message" is held to be a mere play of meanings that cancel each other out. But this polysemic process can only be perceived by a reader willing to remain with a natural logic of representation—the wind driving a cloud, Verlaine suffering physically from the cold—for a longer span of time than is allowed for by Stierle, who wants us to give up any representational reference from the start, without trying out some of the possibilities of a representational reading.

In the second stanza of the sonnet, Stierle is certainly right when he asserts that a *summmum* of incomprehensibility is reached in the lines

> Ici . . .
> Cet immatériel deuil opprime de maints
> Nubiles plis l'astre mûri des lendemains . . .

What on earth (or, for that matter, in heaven) could be these nubile folds that oppress a star or, if one follows Stierle's tempting, because syntactically very Mallarmean suggestion that "maints nubiles plis" by inversion modifies "astre" and not "opprime," what then is this mourning that oppresses a star made up of many nubile folds? The word "pli" is one of the key-symbols of Mallarmé's later vocabulary, too rich to even begin to summarize the series of related meanings it implies. Stierle rightly suggests that one of the meanings refers to the book, the fold being the uncut page that distinguishes the self-reflective volume from the mere information contained in the unfolded, unreflective newspaper. The "nubility" of the book, echoed in the "astre *mûri* des lendemains," helps to identify the star as being the timeless project of the universal Book, the literary paradigm that Mallarmé, half-ironically, half-prophetically, keeps announcing as the *telos* of his and of all literary enterprise. The permanence, the immortality of this Book is the true poetic glory bequeathed to future generations. But "nubile," aside from erotic associations (that can be sacrificed to the economy of our exposition), also suggests the bad etymological but very Mallarmean pun on *nubere* (to marry) and *nubes* (cloud). "Nubiles plis," in a visual synecdoche that is bolder than it is felicitous, underscored by an etymological pun, sees the clouds as folds of vapor about to discharge their rain. The cloud imagery already present in "roc" is thus carried further in the second stanza of the sonnet. This reading, which nowise cancels out the reading of "pli" as book—the syntactical ambivalence of giving "maints nubiles plis" both adjectival and adverbial status is a controlled grammatical device entirely in the spirit of Mallarmé's later style—opens up access to the main theme of the poem: the difference between the false kind of transcendence that bases poetic immortality on the exemplary destiny of the poet considered as a person (in the case of Verlaine, the redeeming sacrifice of the suffering sinner), and authentic poetic immortality that is entirely devoid of any personal circumstances. Mallarmé's prose statements on Verlaine show that this is indeed one of his main concerns with regard to this particular poet, an illustration of his own reflections on the theme of poetic impersonality. The actual person Verlaine, as the first tercet unambiguously states, is now part of the material earth— ". . . il est caché parmi l'herbe, Verlaine"—and far removed from the heavenly constellation of which his work has become a part. The symbol of the false transcendence that tries to rise from the person to the work, from the earthly Verlaine to the poetic text, is the cloud. The misdirected mourning of the contemporaries, the superficial judgments of the journalists, all prevent the true significance of the work from manifesting itself. In the straightforward representational logic of the line, the cloud ("maints nubiles plis") covers up the star ("opprime . . . l'astre") and hides it from sight. In the dramatic action performed by the various symbolic objects, the set of meanings associated with clouds ("roc," "nubiles plis" . . .) denounces the psychological fallacy of confusing the impersonal self of the poetry with the empirical self of the life. Verlaine himself did not share in this mystification, or rather, the correct critical reading of his work shows that his poetry is in fact not a poetry of redemption, sacrifice, or personal transcendence. The *Tombeaux* poems always also contain Mallarmé's own critical interpretation of the other poet's work and he sees Verlaine very much the way Yeats saw William Morris, as a naïvely pagan poet unaware of the tragic, Christian sense of death, a fundamentally happy pastoral poet of earth despite the misery of his existence. In the second part of the sonnet, the imagery shifts from Christian to pagan sources, from the Ascension to the river Styx, with the suggestion that he, Mallarmé, might repeat consciously the experience Verlaine went through in naïve ignorance. Verlaine's death and poetic transfiguration prefigures in a naïve tonality the highly self-conscious repetition of the same experience by Mallarmé himself. Like all true poets, Verlaine is a poet of death, but death for Mallarmé means precisely the discontinuity between the personal self and the voice that speaks in the poetry from the other bank of the river, beyond death.

These brief indications do not begin to do justice to the complexity of this poem or to the depth of the Mallarmean theme linking impersonality with death. They merely confirm that, as one would expect, the sonnet on Verlaine shares the thematic concerns that are present in the poetry and in the prose texts of the same period, including *Un Coup de Dés* with its insistence on the necessary transposition of the sacrificial death from the life into the work. It is important for our argument that these themes can only be reached if one admits the persistent presence, in the poetry, of levels of meaning that

remain representational. The natural image of the cloud covering a star is an indispensable element in the development of the
dramatic action that takes place in the poem. The image of the
poetic work as a star implies that poetic understanding is still,
for Mallarmé, analogous to an act of seeing and therefore best
represented by a natural metaphor of light, like the lamp in
Abrams's title. The poem uses a representational poetics that
remains fundamentally mimetic throughout.

It can be argued that this representational moment is not the
ultimate horizon of Mallarmé's poetry and that, in certain texts
that would probably not include the *Tombeau de Verlaine*, we
move beyond any thematic meaning whatsoever. Even in this
poem, the "ideas" that allow for direct statement, however
subtle and profound, however philosophically valid in their
own right they may be, are not the ultimate *raison d'être* of
the text, but mere pre-text. To say this, however—and the
statement would require many developments and qualifications
—is to say something quite different from Stierle's assertion
that a language of representation is immediately transcended
and replaced by an allegorical, figural language. Only after all
possible representational meanings have been exhausted can one
begin to ask if and by what these meanings have been replaced,
and chances are that this will be nothing as harmless as Stierle's
entirely formal notions of allegory. Up to a very advanced
point, not reached in this poem and perhaps never reached at
all, Mallarmé remains a representational poet as he remains in
fact a poet of the self, however impersonal, disincarnated, and
ironical this self may become in a figure like the "Maître" of
*Un Coup de Dés*. Poetry does not give up its mimetic function
and its dependence on the fiction of a self that easily and at
such little cost.

The implications of this conclusion for the problem of

modernity in the lyric reach further than their apparent scholasticism may at first suggest. For Stierle, following Jauss who himself followed Friedrich, it goes without saying that the crisis of the self and of representation in lyric poetry of the nineteenth and twentieth centuries should be interpreted as a gradual process. Baudelaire continues trends implicitly present in Diderot; Mallarmé (as he himself stated) felt he had to begin where Baudelaire had ended; Rimbaud takes an even further step in opening up the experimentation of the surrealists—in short, the modernity of poetry occurs as a continuous historical movement. This reconciliation of modernity with history in a common genetic process is highly satisfying, because it allows one to be both origin and offspring at the same time. The son understands the father and takes his work a step further, becoming in turn the father, the source of future offspring, "l'astre *mûri* des lendemains," as Mallarmé puts it in a properly genetic imagery of ripening. The process is by no means as easy and spontaneous as it appears in nature: its closest mythological version, the War of the Titans, is far from idyllic. Yet, as far as the idea of modernity is concerned, it remains an optimistic story. Jupiter and his kin may have their share of guilt and sorrow about the fate of Saturn, but they nevertheless are modern men as well as historical figures, linked to a past that they carry within themselves. Their sorrow is a life-giving form of understanding and it integrates the past as an active presence within the future. The literary historian gets a similar satisfaction from a rigorous historical method that remembers the past while he takes part in the excitement of a youthful new present, in the activism of modernity. Such a reconciliation of memory with action is the dream of all historians. In the field of literary studies, the documented modernism of Hans Robert Jauss and his group, who seem to have

no qualms about dating the origins of modernism with historical accuracy, is a good contemporary example of this dream.
In their case, it rests on the assumption that the movement of
lyric poetry away from representation is a historical process
that dates back to Baudelaire as well as being the very movement of modernity. Mallarmé might in all likelihood have
agreed with this, since he himself resorts frequently, and especially in his later works, to images of filial descent, images of
projected futurity which, although no longer founded on organic continuity, nevertheless remain genetic.

With one curious and puzzling exception, however. Many
critics have pointed out that among the various *Tombeaux*
poems paying tribute to his predecessors, the sonnet on Baudelaire is oddly unsatisfying. The subtle critical understanding
that allows Mallarmé to state his kinship as well as his differences with other artists such as Poe, Gautier, Verlaine, or even
Wagner seems to be lacking in the Baudelaire poem. Contrary
to the controlled obscurity of the others, this text may well
contain genuine areas of blindness. In fact, Mallarmé's relationship to Baudelaire is so complex that little of real insight has yet
been said on the bond that united them. The question is not
helped by such lapidary pronouncements as Stierle's assertion
that "Mallarmé began as a pupil of Baudelaire with pastiches of
the *Fleurs du Mal*. His latest poem shows how far he went
beyond his starting point." In the early poems, most of all in
*Hérodiade*, Mallarmé is in fact systematically opposing a certain conception of Baudelaire as a sensuous and subjective poet
—which might well be the limit of his own explicit understanding of Baudelaire at that time—while simultaneously responding, especially in his prose poems, to another, darker
aspect of the later Baudelaire. The two strains remain operative
till the end, the first developing into the main body of his

poetic production, the latter remaining more subterranean but
without ever disappearing altogether. The truly allegorical,
later Baudelaire of the *Petits Poèmes en Prose* never stopped
haunting Mallarmé, though he may have tried to exorcize his
presence. Here was, in fact, the example of a poetry that came
close to being no longer representational but that remained
for him entirely enigmatic. The darkness of this hidden center
obscures later allusions to Baudelaire, including the *Tombeau*
poem devoted to the author of the *Fleurs du Mal*. Far from
being an older kinsman who sent him on his way, Baudelaire,
or, at least, the most significant aspect of Baudelaire, is for him
a dark zone into which he could never penetrate. The same is
true, in different ways, for Rimbaud's and the surrealists' view
of Baudelaire. The understanding of the nonrepresentational,
allegorical element in Baudelaire—and, for that matter, in
Baudelaire's predecessors in romanticism—is very recent and
owes little to Mallarmé or Rimbaud. In terms of the poetics of
representation, the relationship from Baudelaire to so-called
modern poetry is by no means genetic. He is not the father of
modern poetry but an enigmatic stranger that later poets tried
to ignore by taking from him only the superficial themes and
devices which they could rather easily "go beyond." In authentic poets such as Mallarmé, this betrayal caused the slightly
obsessive bad conscience that shines through in his later allusions to Baudelaire. Such a relationship is not the genetic movement of a historical process but more like the uneasy and
shifting border line that separates poetic truth from poetic
falsehood.

It could not have been otherwise, for if one takes the allegorization of poetry seriously and calls it the distinctive characteristic of modernity in the lyric, then all remnants of a
genetic historicism have to be abandoned. When one of the

most significant of modern lyricists, the German poet Paul
Celan, writes a poem about his main predecessor Hölderlin, he
does not write a poem about light but about blindness.[13] The
blindness here is not caused by an absence of natural light but
by the absolute ambivalence of a language. It is a self-willed
rather than a natural blindness, not the blindness of the sooth-
sayer but rather that of Oedipus at Colonus, who has learned
that it is not in his power to solve the enigma of language. One
of the ways in which lyrical poetry encounters this enigma is
in the ambivalence of a language that is representational and
nonrepresentational at the same time. All representational
poetry is always also allegorical, whether it be aware of it or
not, and the allegorical power of the language undermines and
obscures the specific literal meaning of a representation open to
understanding. But all allegorical poetry must contain a representational element that invites and allows for understanding,
only to discover that the understanding it reaches is necessarily
in error. The Mallarmé-Baudelaire relationship is exemplary for
all intra-poetic relationships in that it illustrates the impossi-
bility for a representational and an allegorical poetics to engage
in a mutually clarifying dialectic. Both are necessarily closed
to each other, blind to each other's wisdom. Always again, the

[13] Paul Celan, "Tübingen, Jänner," in *Die Niemandsrose* (Frankfurt a. M., 1963), p. 24. The first stanza of the poem goes as follows:

> Zur Blindheit über—
> redete Augen.
> Ihre—"ein
> Rätsel ist Rein-
> entsprungenes"—, ihre
> Erinnerung an
> schwimmende Hölderlintürme, möwen-
> umschwirrt.

allegorical is made representational, as we saw Jauss and his disciples do when they tried to understand the relationship between mimesis and allegory as a genetic process, forcing into a pattern of continuity that which is, by definition, the negation of all continuity. Or we see ultimate truth being read back into a representation by forcing literal meaning into an allegorical mold, the way Stierle prematurely allegorized a Mallarmé who knew himself to be forever trapped in the deluding appearance of natural images. The question of modernity reveals the paradoxical nature of a structure that makes lyric poetry into an enigma which never stops asking for the unreachable answer to its own riddle. To claim, with Friedrich, that modernity is a form of obscurity is to call the oldest, most ingrained characteristics of poetry modern. To claim that the loss of representation is modern is to make us again aware of an allegorical element in the lyric that had never ceased to be present, but that is itself necessarily dependent on the existence of an earlier allegory and thus the negation of modernity. The worst mystification is to believe that one can move from representation to allegory, or vice versa, as one moves from the old to the new, from father to son, from history to modernity. Allegory can only blindly repeat its earlier model, without final understanding, the way Celan repeats quotations from Hölderlin that assert their own incomprehensibility. The less we understand a poet, the more he gets compulsively misinterpreted and oversimplified, made to say the opposite of what he actually said, the better the chances that he is truly modern, that is, different from what we—mistakenly—think we are ourselves. This would make Baudelaire into a truly modern French poet, Hölderlin into a truly modern German poet, Wordsworth and Yeats perhaps into truly modern English poets.

## THE PROGRAM

I. Forms of the Lyric, at 9:30 A.M.
*Directed by Reuben A. Brower, Harvard University*

Tues.  The Renaissance Lyric: Drab and Golden
*G. K. Hunter, University of Warwick*

Wed.  Lyric and Modernity
*Paul De Man, The Johns Hopkins University*

Thurs.  Wildness of Logic in Lyric Poetry
*William H. Pritchard, Amherst College*

Fri.  The Re-invented Poem: George Herbert's Alternatives
*Helen Vendler, Boston University*

II. Literary Realism, at 11:00 A.M.
*Directed by Norman S. Grabo, University of California, Berkeley*

Tues.  Is the Problem of Literary Realism a Pseudo-Problem?
*Morse Peckham, University of South Carolina*

Thurs.  Tolstoy and Realism
*John Henry Raleigh, University of California, Berkeley*

Fri.  The *Reality* of Literature
*Eliseo Vivas, Rockford College*

III. Literary Magazines and Literary Change, at 1:45 P.M.
*Directed by Monroe K. Spears, Rice University*

Tues.  Panel Discussion
*Allen Tate; John Palmer, Yale Review; Monroe K. Spears*

Wed.    British Literary Magazines, 1910–1930
        *Jacob Korg, University of Maryland*
Fri.    Little Magazines and Large Causes
        *Reed Whittemore, University of Maryland*

IV. The Confessional Mode: Revealing and Concealing, at
    3:15 P.M.
    *Directed by Norman N. Holland, State University of
    New York at Buffalo*
        Tues.    Chutzpah and Pudeur
                 *Leslie Fiedler, State University of New
                 York at Buffalo*
        Thurs.   Proust and the Art of Incompletion
                 *Leo Bersani, Rutgers University*
        Fri.     The Self as Performance
                 *Richard Poirier, Rutgers University*

V. Prize Essays
    *Directed by Irvin Ehrenpreis, University of Virginia*
        Wednesday, 11:00 A.M. Coleridge and Wordsworth's
        "Whelming Tide"
            *A. Reeve Parker, Cornell University*
        Thursday, 1:45 P.M. The Confessional Increment
            *David Goldknopf, Bennett College*

Ruth M. Adams, Wellesley College; Sister Agnes, Chestnut Hill College; W. T. Albrecht, Colgate University; G. S. Alleman, Rutgers University at Newark; Marcia Allentuck, City College, CUNY; Valborg Anderson, Brooklyn College, CUNY; Sister Ann Edward, Chestnut Hill College; L. M. Antalis, Columbia University; Stanford Apseloff, Kent State University; Frederick Asals, New College, University of Toronto; Heather Asals, York University

G. W. Bahlke, Middlebury College; Virginia P. Barber, Duke University; Richard E. Barbieri, Emmanuel College; Rev. J. Robert Barth, Canisius College; Phyllis Bartlett, Queens College, CUNY; Rev. John E. Becker, St. Louis University; Alice R. Bensen, Eastern Michigan University; Bernard Benstock, Kent State University; Leo Bersani, Rutgers University; Major Joseph A. Berthelot, United States Air Force Academy; Warner Berthoff, Harvard University; John B. Beston, City College, CUNY; Siegmund A. E. Betz, Edgecliff College; Murray J. K. Biggs, University of Connecticut; Whitney Blake, Oxford University Press; Haskell M. Block, Brooklyn College, CUNY; Max Bluestone, University of Massachusetts at Boston; Anne C. Bolgan, University of Western Ontario; Sister M. Bonaventure, Nazareth College; George Bornstein, Rutgers University; Rev. John D. Boyd, Fordham University; Alan T. Bradford, Connecticut College; Frank Brady, CUNY; Helene M. Brewer, Queens College, CUNY; James Brophy, Iona College; Reuben A. Brower, Harvard University; Kenneth A. Bruffee, Brooklyn College, CUNY; Audrey Brune, Sir George Williams University; Robert B. Burlin, Bryn Mawr College; Glenn S. Burne, Kent State University; Sister M. Vincentia Burns, o.p., Albertus Magnus College; Guy Burton, Ridgewood, New Jersey; George E. Bush, St. Francis College; Lois Byrns, Stout State University

Lalox Cadley, Princeton University Press; John Cameron, Amherst College; Ronald Campbell, Harcourt, Brace & World, Inc.; James

Van Dyck Card, Old Dominion University; James F. Carens, Bucknell University; Donald S. Cheney, Jr., University of Massachusetts; Kent Christensen, Upsala College; Ralph Ciancio, Skidmore College; James L. Clifford, Columbia University; Sister Anne Gertrude Coleman, College of St. Elizabeth; Arthur N. Collins, State University of New York at Albany; Rowland L. Collins, University of Rochester; David B. Comer, Georgia Institute of Technology; Anthony Covatta, Columbia University; David Cowden, Swarthmore College; Patricia Craddock, Goucher College; G. Armour Craig, Amherst College; Robert P. Creed, University of Massachusetts at Amherst; Marion Cumpiano, University of Puerto Rico

Irene G. Dash, Columbia University; Winifred M. Davis, Columbia University; Robert A. Day, Queens College, CUNY; Paul De Man, The Johns Hopkins University; Talbot E. Donaldson, Columbia University; Charles T. Dougherty, University of Missouri, St. Louis; Thomas F. Dunn, Canisius College

Delbert L. Earisman, Upsala College; Benjamin W. Early, Mary Washington College; Thomas R. Edwards, Rutgers University; Irvin Ehrenpreis, University of Virginia; George P. Elliott, Syracuse University; William Elton, Graduate Center, CUNY; Martha W. England, Queens College, CUNY; David V. Erdman, State University of New York at Stony Brook; Sister Marie Eugénie, Immaculata College; Robert O. Evans, University of Kentucky; William Clay Evans, Occidental College

N. N. Feltes, York University, Toronto; Leslie Fiedler, State University of New York at Buffalo; Stanley Eugene Fish, University of California, Berkeley; Edward G. Fletcher, University of Texas; French Fogle, Claremont Graduate School; Arthur L. Ford, Lebanon Valley College; George H. Ford, University of Rochester; Robert D. Foulke, Trinity College; Charles E. Frank, Illinois College; Glenn Frankenfield, Farmington State College; Morris Freedman, University of Maryland; Albert B. Friedman, Claremont Graduate School; Northrop Frye, Victoria College, University of Toronto

Col. Jesse C. Gatlin, United States Air Force Academy; Marilyn S. Gaull, Temple University; Blanche Gelfant, Upstate Medical Center, State University of New York; Carol Gesner, Berea College; Walker Gibson, University of Massachusetts at Amherst; Jessie Gilmer, University of Denver; Richard L. Goldfarb, York University, Toronto; David Goldknopf, State University College of New York at New Paltz; Norman S. Grabo, University of California, Berkeley; Matthew Grace, Université de Clermont; Thomas J. Grace, Talladega College; John E. Grant, University of Iowa; Richard L. Greene, Wesleyan University; M. E. Grenander, State University of New York at Albany; Ira Grushow, Franklin and Marshall College; John C. Guilds, University of South Carolina; Allen Guttmann, Amherst College

Jean H. Hagstrum, Northwestern University; Claire Hahn, Fordham University; Gordon S. Haight, Yale University; Ulrich Halfmann, Universität Freiburg; Robert Halsband, Columbia University; Richard Harrier, New York University; Francis R. Hart, University of Virginia; John A. Hart, Carnegie-Mellon University; Lorena L. Hart, University of Virginia; Joan E. Hartman, Queens College, CUNY; Carol A. Hawkes, Finch College; Ann L. Hayes, Carnegie-Mellon University; Allen T. Hazen, Columbia University; Roger B. Henkle, Brown University; Hugh L. Hennedy, St. Francis College; Lucille Herbert, York University, Toronto; James Lewis Hill, Michigan State University; Rev. William Bernard Hill, University of Scranton; Charles C. Hobbs, Carson-Newman College; Daniel Hoffman, University of Pennsylvania; Norman H. Holland, State University of New York at Buffalo; Frank S. Hook, Lehigh University; Vivian C. Hopkins, State University of New York at Albany; George Hunter, University of California, Berkeley; Samuel Hynes, Northwestern University

Sears Jayne, Brown University; Samuel F. Johnson, Columbia University; Dillon Johnston, St. Lawrence University; B. W. Jones, Carleton University; Leah E. Jordan, West Chester State College; Sister Joseph Immaculate, St. Joseph's College for Women

Rosemary Kammerer, Edgecliff College; Sister Melinda Keane, Rosemont College; Constance D. Kehoe, Wheelock College; Walter B. Kelly, Mary Washington College; Sister Eileen Kennedy, College of St. Elizabeth; Karl Kiralis, University of Houston; Maurine H.

Klein, County College of Morris; H. L. Kleinfield, C. W. Post College; Mary E. Knapp, Albertus Magnus College; Jacob Korg, University of Maryland; Joaquin C. Kuhn, St. Michael's College, University of Toronto; George Kummer, Case Western Reserve University

Penny Laurans, Harvard University; Katharine Kyes Leab, Columbia University Press; Lewis Leary, University of North Carolina; James T. Livingston, Drury College; Joseph P. Lovering, Canisius College; Sister Alice Lubin, College of St. Elizabeth; Richard S. Lyons, Oakland University

Marion Mabey, Wells College; Isabel MacCaffrey, Tufts University; Charles McCann, Evergreen State College; Terence J. McKenzie, United States Coast Guard Academy; Richard A. Macksey, The Johns Hopkins University; Elizabeth T. McLaughlin, Bucknell University; Reta A. Madsen, Webster College; Sister C. E. Maguire, Newton College of the Sacred Heart; Alice S. Mandanis, Catholic University; Jeff Daniel Marion, Carson-Newman College; Sister Catherine Regina Marski, s.c., St. John's University; Louis L. Martz, Yale University; John Kelly Mathison, University of Wyoming; Neill Megaw, University of Texas; John A. Meixner, Rice University; Donald C. Mell, Jr., University of Delaware; Caroline Mercer, Vassar College; John Merrow, Virginia State College; John H. Middendorf, Columbia University; J. Hillis Miller, The Johns Hopkins University; Robert D. Moynihan, State University of New York at Oneonta; William T. Moynihan, University of Connecticut; Sister Elizabeth Marian Murphy, College of Mount St. Vincent; Philip Murphy, Franklin and Marshall College

William Nelson, Columbia University; John M. Nesselhof, Wells College; Rev. William T. Noon, Le Moyne College

Paul E. O'Connell, Winthrop Publishers, Inc.; J. Donald O'Hara, University of Connecticut; Rev. Joseph E. O'Neill, Fordham University; Mother Thomas Aquinas O'Reilly, o.s.u., College of New Rochelle; James M. Osborn, Yale University; Charles A. Owen, Jr., University of Connecticut

Ward Pafford, Valdosta State College; Stephen C. Paine, Bradley University; Sister Florence Pakenham, College of St. Elizabeth;

John Palmer, *Yale Review;* Reeve Parker, Cornell University; Harry Pauley, State College, Shippensburg, Pennsylvania; Richard Pearce, Wheaton College; Roy Harvey Pearce, University of California, San Diego; Norman Holmes Pearson, Yale University; Morse Peckham, University of South Carolina; Marjorie Perloff, Catholic University; Donald Petersen, State University College at Oneonta; Henry H. Peyton, Memphis State University; Sanford Pinsker, Franklin and Marshall College; Richard Poirier, Rutgers University; Annis Pratt, Spelman College; William C. Pratt, Miami University; Robert O. Preyer, Brandeis University; Jonathan Reeve Price, Washington Square College, New York University; Martin Price, Yale University; William Pritchard, Amherst College; Max Putzel, University of Connecticut

Richard E. Quaintance, Jr., Rutgers University

Norman Rabkin, University of California, Berkeley; John Henry Raleigh, University of California, Berkeley; Paul Ramsey, University of Tennessee, Chattanooga; Donald H. Reiman, The Carl H. Pforzheimer Library; G. D. Richards, Skidmore College; Leo Rockas, Briarcliff College; Edward J. Rose, University of Alberta; Shirley Rose, University of Alberta; Sister Rose Bernard Donna, C.S.J., College of Saint Rose; H. B. Rouse, University of Arkansas; Rebecca D. Ruggles, Brooklyn College, CUNY; A. LaVonne Ruoff, University of Illinois; Sister Mary Paton Ryan, R.S.M., Yale University

Maire J. Said, Barnard College; Phillips Salman, Cleveland State University; Gaetano F. Santa Lucia, St. Francis College; Sister Patricia Sauer, R.S.H.M., Marymount Manhattan College; Paul Sawyer, Bradley University; Bernard N. Schilling, University of Rochester; Lillian Schlissel, Brooklyn College; Helene Maria Schnabel, New York, New York; H. T. Schultz, Dartmouth College; Susan Field Senneff, Columbia University; Richard Sexton, Fordham University; F. Parvin Sharpless, Germantown Friends School; Catherine M. Shaw, University of Illinois; Norman Silverstein, Queens College, CUNY; Sister Mary Francis Slattery, Mount Saint Vincent-on-Hudson; Ann Smith, Dalhousie University; Barbara Herrnstein Smith, Bennington College; Rowland Smith, Dalhousie University; Thomas H.

Smith, State University of New York at Albany; Nelle Smither, Douglass College; Susan Snyder, Swarthmore College; Ian Sowton, Atkinson College; Monroe K. Spears, Rice University; Mark Spilka, Brown University; Stan Stanko, Edmonton, Alberta, Canada; M. K. Starkman, Queens College, CUNY; Mary Jane Stephenson, Coker College; Herbert Stern, Wabash College; A. Wilber Stevens, Prescott College; Philip Stevick, Temple University; Fred Stockholder, University of British Columbia; Donald R. Stoddard, Skidmore College; Mary Sullivan, Saint Xavier College; Maureen Sullivan, University of Pennsylvania; Joseph H. Summers, University of Rochester; John Sutherland, Colby College; Donald R. Swanson, Upsala College

Allen Tate, Sewanee, Tennessee; Mary Olive Thomas, Georgia State College; Sister Thomas Marion, Nazareth College; R. J. Thompson, Canisius College; Eva Touster, Peabody College; Mary Curtis Tucker, Marietta, Georgia; Susan J. Turner, Vassar College

Samson O. A. Ullmann, Union College; John Unterecker, Columbia University

V. W. Valentine, University of South Florida; R. T. Van Arsdel, University of Puget Sound; Ruth M. Vande Kieft, Queens College, CUNY; Helen Vendler, Boston University; Howard P. Vincent, Kent State University; Eliseo Vivas, Rockford College

Eugene M. Waith, Yale University; Joseph J. Waldmeir, Michigan State University; Janet Warner, York University, Toronto; John P. Watkins, State College, California, Pennsylvania; Herbert Weil, Jr., University of Connecticut; Helen Weinfurter, Saint Xavier College; Sister Mary Anthony Weinig, Rosemont College; Jeanne K. Welcher, C. W. Post College; Sister Julia Marie Weser, College of Mount St. Vincent; Sister E. White, Newton College of the Sacred Heart; Robert L. White, York University, Toronto; Reed Whittemore, University of Maryland; Joseph Wiesenfarth, F.S.C., Manhattan College; Alan Wilde, Temple University; Maurita Willett, University of Illinois; Ora William, California State College at Long Beach; Dorothy M. Willis, New Haven, Connecticut; Patricia Wilson, St. John's University; W. K. Wimsatt, Yale University; Calhoun Winton, University of South Carolina; James N. Wise,

Newark College of Engineering; Carl Woodring, Columbia University; Samuel H. Woods, Jr., Oklahoma State University

James Dean Young, Georgia Institute of Technology

Steven A. Zemelman, Amherst College; Curt A. Zimansky, University of Iowa; D. E. Zipperer, Rego Park, New York